No Cheating, No Dying

I Had a Good Marriage.
Then I Tried to Make It Better.

Elizabeth Weil

Scribner

New York   London   Toronto   Sydney   New Delhi

SCRIBNER
A Division of Simon & Schuster, Inc.
1230 Avenue of the Americas
New York, NY 10020

First Scribner hardcover edition February 2012

SCRIBNER and design are registered trademarks of The Gale Group, Inc., used under license
by Simon & Schuster, Inc., the publisher of this work.

For information about special discounts for bulk purchases, please contact Simon &
Schuster Special Sales at 1-866-506-1949 or business@simonandschuster.com.

The Simon & Schuster Speakers Bureau can bring authors to your live event.
For more information or to book an event contact the Simon & Schuster Speakers Bureau
at 1-866-248-3049 or visit our website at www.simonspeakers.com.

Designed by Carla Jayne Jones

Manufactured in the United States of America

10   9   8   7   6   5   4   3   2   1

ISBN 978-1-4391-6824-0
ISBN 978-1-4391-6826-4 (ebook)

Portions of this work were previously published in altered form as "Married (Happily) with
Issues" in *The New York Times Magazine,* December 1, 2009.

For Dan

Contents

No Cheating,
No Dying

1
The Project

I have a good marriage.

I had a good marriage before I spent a year improving it, and I have a good marriage now. In fact, my marriage is better, truly better. Although not in the ways I'd expected.

When I set out to improve my marriage, I assumed that *better* would look like a Photoshopped version of *good*: essentially unchanged, unsightly elements gone. Dan would no longer butcher headless, skinless pigs and goats on our kitchen island. I would not tidy up, literally and psychologically, by shoving junk in drawers. We would quit outsourcing the production of our children's religious identities to our parents. We'd stop vibing—yes, *vibing,* we used that word—our bank balances, spending more when we felt flush, less when we felt broke. Instead I got a better marriage in the "before enlightenment, chop wood carry water; after enlightenment, chop wood carry water" sense. I feel humbled, grateful, and transformed, and Dan is still leaving single brown socks (how to tell if they're dirty or clean?) strewn about the house.

The first time Dan and I discussed the possibility of a better marriage we were lying in bed, under our white duvet, amid our white walls, in that little sanctuary of peace and purity that Dan had built for us in our flimsy, hundred-year-old earthquake shack of a house. I believed in marriage. I *liked* being married. But I did not feel expert at it. Shortly after our wedding, nine years prior, we'd started to joke that we needed to take more advantage of being two people, that we really shouldn't do our errands together, write for the same editors, read the same magazines. Back then, Dan had felt alarmed, nearly panicked, that some nights we'd sprawl together on the couch reading our then-still-separate subscriptions to *The New Yorker*. Weren't lovers supposed to maintain, even exaggerate, differences? Certainly his happily married parents had.

I was an even less likely candidate than Dan for a wholly merged life. One of my more telling memories of myself as a young woman and of how unbending I was in love happened the evening a new boyfriend wanted to make me a cilantro-lime pesto, and instead of walking with him on that warm spring evening to buy limes, I suggested he run the errand alone. By the time I met Dan, at age twenty-eight, I'd shed some of that rigidity. I knew more about who I was, so I felt more comfortable being swayed. But nearly a decade into marriage, and sincerely hoping to remain married to Dan for many decades more, I did not understand how much I should be swayed by my husband. What algorithm should determine how much I tipped over into the warm bath of our union and how much of myself to keep separate, outside?

Since our wedding, Dan and I had been bumbling along, more or less successfully, with two basic ground rules: no cheating and no dying. We spoke these rules out loud to each other. We considered their breakages the only trespasses our marriage could not survive. But that night, under our white duvet, as I lay next to Dan's warm and increasingly muscled body, I started wondering why we were being so cavalier. Why weren't we caring more for our marriage, making it as strong as it could be? Dan is really the very best thing that's happened in my life. He squints like Clint Eastwood. He calls me "darling." He'd cook me three meals a day if I let him (which I don't; again, the question of independence). He's a great conversationalist and he makes me feel like one of the more interesting people on earth. So why were we *bumbling*? Why weren't we being more deliberate? I've never been one to leave well enough alone, nor have I ever believed that marriage is binary—that one moment you're single and the next you're not, some alchemy happening at the altar. I've always believed that you get married, truly married, slowly, over time, through all the dental plaque you inadvertently flick into each other's faces; through all the sunsets you watch on remote Baja beaches after you've locked your keys in your rental car, again; through all the near-hypothermic panic attacks because you decided it would be a good idea to swim together from Alcatraz to San Francisco; through all the frozen pig skulls your spouse power saws in half (in order to make pork stock); through all the pain, tears, and absurdity; through small and large moments you never expected to happen and certainly didn't plan to endure.

But then you do: You endure.

That night, for dinner, I endured a deep-fried pig's tail. (Same pig, opposite end.) Some other wife might have endured the NFL. And as I lay next to Dan, later, feeling gustatorily put out, I started wondering why I was being so passive. Not in the sense that I wasn't fighting back. Why wasn't I applying myself more to being a spouse?

I loved Dan utterly. I even made him say this aloud—*Lizzy loves me utterly*—whenever he felt depressed. My marriage was the very center of my life. Sure, we'd taken some hits and suffered some losses, enough to know life and love are fragile. But none had driven a major wedge, at least as far as we acknowledged. So we just kept cruising, promising each other we would not cheat and we would not die, working off the lazy theory: *so far so good.*

This motivational soft spot around marriage was not unique to my own. Most of my peers had spent their twenties and thirties *applying* themselves: to school, work, sports, health, friendship, and, most recently, parenting—which in my case meant trying to figure out how best to raise an eight-year-old so lost in her dreams of *The Secret Garden* that she falls off the kitchen stool while eating breakfast, and a five-year-old so outrageous she's on track to be the next Sarah Silverman. But in this critical area—marriage—we'd shrugged and turned away. I wanted to understand why. I wanted to stop accepting this. Dan, too, had spent his twenties and thirties working tirelessly—okay, obsessively—at skill acquisition. Over the course of our eleven years together, he'd taught himself to be a meticulous carpenter and excellent, if catastrophically messy, chef. He'd buy mountainous stacks of books. Read. Take notes. Practice. Read more. Take more notes. Practice more. Repeat. In this way he'd learned to sweat pipe, run electrical wiring, hang drywall, cut stringers for stairs, salt cod, cure pancetta, build sourdough starter, reduce fifty dollars' worth of veal bones down to two cups of stock. On the night in question, Dan had been working on his so-called "fitness unit," studying the obscure Soviet-era weight-training manuals of Tudor Bompa, in hopes of transforming his already-reasonably-fit forty-one-year-old body into that of a young marine. My point here is that this man, my husband, was not an if-it's-not-broke-don't-fix-it kind of person. Yet he, too, shared the seemingly ubiquitous aversion to the concept of looking inside and trying to improve our marriage, and doing so not because our marriage was in crisis but just because marriage is so important and prone to drift.

That night, in bed, the image that came to mind, and that I shared with Dan, was that I'd been viewing our marriage like the waves on the ocean—a fact of life, determined by the sandbars below, shaped by destiny and the universe, not by me. And this, suddenly, seemed ridiculous. I am not a fatalistic person. In my twenties I even believed that people made their own luck. Part of the luck I believed I'd made for myself arrived in the form of Dan himself, three days after I'd moved to San Francisco, in the spring of 1998. Meeting this rugged freckled redhead was beyond the best-case scenario I'd envisioned for a move I'd worked diligently, of course, to make quite smooth. Before leaving Chicago, where I'd been living, I'd arranged to rent a small office in a group space for San Francisco writers called the Grotto. Every Tuesday these mostly young, mostly single writers met at a bar called Mars. That first Tuesday, in walked Dan.

He looked like he'd just climbed out of the ocean, as in not even showered before pulling on his jeans. His nose was straight, sunburned, and peeling. He had salt caked on his eyelashes and in his hair. He was tall, angular, calm, and handsome, and when he talked he covered his mouth with a hand, to hide the gap between his teeth. But I liked this—his vulnerability, his apparently thin skin. I thought it made him approachable. He had blue eyes, startlingly clear, which he also hid behind ancient gold-rimmed glasses. They were the most beautiful eyes I'd ever seen.

Just that afternoon, Dan told me, he'd gotten "bageled," meaning he'd caught no waves, while surfing Ocean Beach.

"I know, it's pretty pathetic, right?" he said, nodding, covering his mouth, seeing if he could recruit me to agree.

"No, it's not pathetic at all," I said. "Or is it? I mean, I don't really know."

"Believe me, it's pathetic," Dan said. He was a big hunky insecure mess.

Dan was also a catch. A few years earlier he'd written a surf memoir called *Caught Inside,* and for this, in a review, he'd been anointed an "ontologist of dudedom, Henry David Thoreau doing aerials on a fiberglass board." Dan didn't tell me about the book. Mostly he wanted me to know that prior to getting bageled he'd spent the day depressed, lying on the floor of his room, staring at the glow-in-the-dark stars the previous tenant had glued to the ceiling. I learned about the memoir the following day when I walked up Valencia Street and bought *Caught Inside* myself. I didn't read the memoir for months. I was too scared. I just memorized the jacket copy and stared at Dan's author photo.

He stood on a dune, gazing into the sun, looking self-conscious and endearing.

That spring I'd left Chicago because I wanted, needed, something to happen in my life. I've always tended toward stability while fearing boredom, so every few years I give myself a swift kick. Before San Francisco my plan had been to move to South Africa to witness the post-apartheid truth commissions. This struck me as a good way to solve two core problems: my feeling that I didn't know anything about anything (which I now see was related to the problem of being twenty-six) and my increasing annoyance with the chirpy magazine articles I wrote to pay my rent. But then I heard about a man building a civilian spaceship in the Mojave Desert, and, wanting change more than I wanted anything in particular, I decided to write a book about him. I loaded my clothes into my Honda Civic, bought a Johnny Cash box set, and pointed west. En route I blew my head gasket and skidded out in a spring blizzard in Donner Pass. Still I kept moving forward—my specialty and downfall—hoping to leave behind the last traces of what I considered to be an embarrassing youth.

Like the textiles. God, the textiles. I'd grown up in Wellesley, Massachusetts, in a home filled with awful fabrics—pastel chevron-striped sofas, rust velour loungers, a canary yellow pleather couch. Worse, I seemed to have inherited the bad textile gene. Before my junior year in college my mother drove me to Bob's Discount Furniture, where she allowed me to pick out a pink-and-white-striped La-Z-Boy chair. I felt fantastic about the chair until I moved it into my dorm and saw with hideous clarity that I carried the family curse. As I drove west from Chicago I committed myself to a lifelong plan to thwart the gene's expression: I'd buy only wood furniture. The plan worked for a couple of years.

A few days after meeting Dan, I thought up an excuse to call him. A friend was visiting from Chicago. We'd driven to the Marin Headlands, looking for a gorgeous hike, but ended up in Muir Woods with the tourists on a paved path. My ontologist, surely, could deliver me from this problem.

"That's it, huh?" Dan said, teasing, when I phoned. "You just thought maybe I could suggest a pretty hike?"

"It's true!" I protested. Or at least it was partly true.

The next Tuesday, at Mars, Dan arrived flecked with salt again.

"So, did you make it to Coyote Ridge?" he asked.

"Yes, thank you. Did you get bageled?"

He laughed, eyes bioluminescent. Then he put me out of my misery and asked me on a date.

Everyone has a theory of marriage; few of them agree: The happiest marriages are based on the least romantic expectations; the happiest marriages are maintained by spouses who cling to rosy lenses and insist on holding their partners in delusionally high regard. In a happy marriage, the focus is inward, the relationship comes first; in a happy marriage, each spouse encourages the other to attain individual goals.

One popular, if superstitious, belief is that you can learn a lot from people's origin stories. Mine with Dan is built on the idea of destiny. Dan's version rests on destiny, too, though he skips my move from Chicago and our meeting at Mars and starts instead the following Friday, on our first date, when, over Knob Creek whiskey, he told me about his soon-to-be-published novel and how, in it, the protagonist takes advice on how to pick up girls from an article called "How to Get the Love You Deserve," published in *Rolling Stone*.

I set down my drink, unnerved. "You're kidding, right?"

"No, why?"

"I wrote that article."

Dan stared, thrilled, his self-deprecating guard dropped.

A month later, Dan read from his novel at A Clean Well-Lighted Place for Books. The house was packed with his surf buddies, his warm and gracious family, and the former Berkeley High School water polo team. Dan held the room rapt—breaking away from the funny stories he'd written to tell funny tangents not in the book. He looked fantastic, in his faded Levi's and plaid shirt, and he was very charming. So much so that as I left, a man I knew from college yanked my elbow and said, "Oh my god, he'll date you?"

I pretended, in the moment, to be offended. But to be honest I felt the same way: stunned that Dan would throw his lot in with me, amazed that he was mine. Eleven years later, I still felt this: proud, nearly giddy, to be his wife. Of course as I lay in bed, digesting the pig's tail, that giddiness was buried beneath the mess in the kitchen, the ever-toppling stacks of weight-training books, the small domestic disturbances that often appear huge, the way a thumbnail held up to the night sky might cover the moon. But I loved Dan. I loved him more than I did at the start. Plus now we had two kids, two jobs, a house, a tenant, a sprawling local extended family—what Nikos Kazantzakis describes in *Zorba the Greek* as "the full catastrophe." And I was going to be passive about how our union worked out?

Our children, Hannah and Audrey, bless their klutzy selves, were no longer desperately needy. Our careers had stabilized. We'd survived gutting our own house. Viewed darkly, one could say I feared stasis. (For the first time in our lives together, neither Dan nor I was trying to finish a book, or pregnant, or nursing, or reeling from a lost pregnancy, or living in a construction zone.) More positively, I had energy for Dan once again. Whatever the case—undoubtedly some of both—I borrowed Dan's furious skill-acquisition method. I decided to apply myself to my marriage by any and all means. I also took notes, all of which turned into what you're reading here. I quickly learned that my idea was sound, if a bit unusual. The average couple is unhappily married six years before presenting at therapy, at which point, according to *The Science of Clinical Psychology,* the marital therapist's job is often "less like the emergency room physician who is called upon to set a fracture that happened a few hours ago and more like a general practitioner who is asked to treat a patient who broke his or her leg several months ago and then continued to hobble around on it; we have to attend not only to the broken bone but to the swelling and the bruising, the sore hip and foot, and the infection that ensued."

I didn't want to become one of those people. I had a strong tendency just to keep marching forward in life and I didn't want that to lead me to become like Sandra Tsing Loh, a woman I identified with and admired. She described in the *Atlantic Monthly* leaving her husband of twenty years, how she sat in some therapist's office, realizing that she lacked "the strength"—more rightly, the will?—"to 'work on' falling in love again" with her marriage. Because just as I believed that marriages formed slowly over time, I also believed they broke that way. People drifted. Dan and I had drifted. Needs diverged. Thus far Dan and I had managed always to return to each other. But what if someday the husband, the wife, the proverbial falcon started flying off a little farther than usual? At some point the center—the marriage—cannot hold. There's only one direction to go: out. No coming back.

We'd been married nearly a decade, yet we knew so little. Nobody else seemed to know much, either. When I looked around my block or my city, among my family and friends, I found many happy marriages, filled with qualities I envied, but not a single one for which I'd want to trade. Some had combustive chemistry but cycled through burnout and renewal. Others had financial security but had traded footloose selves for traditional roles, and that seemed hard, too. Becoming parents had helped nobody, and the standard remedies—the date nights, the weekend getaways—often felt cosmetic and under-gunned, like opening a beautifully wrapped and ribboned box to find one's own clothes. I felt changed by marriage, shaped by marriage, mostly for the better. But it also scared me. Dan was my "elected homeland of the heart," to borrow a phrase from Madeleine Kamman's *When French Women Cook*, one of his favorite books. I needed him. He understood me *and* he loved me—nobody else in the world offered both. Still the images of marriage I found most arresting I also found most troubling. Along with *Who's*

Afraid of Virginia Woolf?, I adored John Updike's *The Maples Stories,* stories in which twelve years of marriage feel "almost too long" and Joan and Richard Maples are jaded and hard. In "Twin Beds in Rome," the couple flies to Italy to "cure or kill" their union. The whole vacation is a gauntlet thrown. "You're such a nice woman," Richard says to Joan as they unpack in their hotel. "I can't understand why I'm so miserable with you."

I didn't want this narrative—nobody did. Still, Dan was not completely enthusiastic about my marriage improvement concept, at least at first. He feared—not mistakenly, it turned out—that marriage is not great terrain for overachievers. That first night, in our bedroom, he met my marriage-as-waves-on-the-ocean analogy with the veiled threat of California ranch-hand wisdom: If you're going to poke around the bushes, you'd better be prepared to scare out some snakes.

2
Nuptials

Before I got married I didn't put much stock in psychology. It struck me as defeatist, too anchored in the past, a trick for making tidy stories out of sloppy lives. So I didn't attach meaning to Dan's desire to fire our wedding officiant (the most obvious—possibly the only—man for the job: a Jewish judge who knew both families). Nor did I ponder the unsynchronous outfits we chose for our wedding, which took place on July 1, 2000, in Olema, California, a few rolling hills away from the Point Reyes seashore. I wore a long white dress that cost more than our crappy Subaru wagon is presently worth. Dan wore his gold wire-rimmed glasses held together by a paper clip, and a brown suit he'd bought against his will with the aid of a Nordstrom's salesclerk who'd grown fed up with Dan buying suits and bringing them back. Before the brown suit Dan had purchased and returned many "wedding costumes," as he called them, each evoking a different fantasy of who he'd be as a married man. The first was a slick Zegna, on sale, the color of summer grass (by which Dan meant burnt tan, not kelly green; summer grass in California). In it, Dan, as husband, would be very rich and extremely hard charging, a Los Angeles mogul in a Porsche. The second was another Zegna, full price and richly hued like the forest floor. For this one, Dan justified the expense by saying that he'd wear it all the time. He'd be a dreamy Tuscan roaming his winery, in espadrilles, or possibly huaraches, shirt open, trailed by beautiful peaceful children. Except Dan would be in the Mission District of San Francisco.

The final suit elicited no such fantasies. It was simple, well cut, reasonably priced, the only suit Dan's ever owned. Granted, Dan owned it because the clerk neglected to hear the final "Please, cancel the suit" message Dan left while the brown two-piece waited, chalked up, for the tailor. But now that the brown suit hangs in our closet, and now that I'm open psychologically to what it might mean, I believe it was the perfect outfit for entering a stable, happy marriage. I do not believe the same about my dress. My dress was a lovely delusion. It now sits, missing a button, in a box in our basement. At our wedding I was thirty and Dan was thirty-two years old.

Ours had been a joyous but rocky start, and one that had a deeper impact than I'd realized. The same day that I'd blown my head gasket and skidded crossing Donner Pass, Dan had broken off a yearlong relationship with an emotionally sadistic and sexually self-aggrandizing woman. (Or at least that's how she sounded in the stories Dan told me. I never met her.) She'd said mean things to him and in our first few months together, while working her out of his system, Dan passed the favor along to me.

"I don't like your glasses."

"Why do you kiss like *that?*"

I brushed these comments aside and waited for the "real" Dan, the charmingly compulsive gap-toothed nodder, to return. But excuses do not lay the best foundation for a marriage. (Memory, I've been forced to accept, preserves wounds, not their justifications.) Nor was our union helped by the fact that during our courtship Dan was under contract to write a book about hiking California's 211-mile John Muir Trail, which for a while turned into a book about *not* hiking the Muir Trail and instead exploring the great indoors, à la Geoff Dyer's *Out of Sheer Rage*. Dan's book, during our engagement, then morphed into an erotic bildungsroman about his nightmare ex-girlfriend, at one point ballooning to five hundred pages and including references to every woman he'd ever slept with. I convinced myself to accept the bachelor party impulse behind this. But by the time the book came out Dan and I would be married. Was I supposed to attend his readings? I'm proud to a fault. Letting go of my pride scared me. I did not understand how marriage was supposed to function in times of real conflict. When you can't meet your own needs and those of your spouse, how do you choose?

Still I never doubted that Dan and I should be together. Snide remarks about my eyeglasses and other indications to the contrary, I felt the inevitability of our union when we just had filaments of evidence that it made sense, like the afternoon we sat on the sunny stairs, in front of my apartment on Dorland Street, and I told Dan I was a cynic drawn to believers, and he looked at me like a twelve-year-old who's just realized the tomboy who plays shortstop on his Little League team is actually a beautiful girl. I also felt that essential rightness, six weeks later, when Dan and I sat on a grassy knoll in Dolores Park and broke up. Following the *Rolling Stone* date, we'd started seeing each other daily, sometimes more than once: tea after lunch, maybe a post-work run, falafel for dinner at Truly Mediterranean, back when food for Dan was just fuel. But now, in Dolores Park, high on a berm overlooking the downtown and the Bay, Dan started blathering about how he didn't trust himself to be dating anybody at all.

"I mean, I always meet someone, I go on a date, I go on another date, and it's like every time you sleep together you're sewing another little stitch between your hearts, so that even if you never meant to get in a big relationship, it makes this big, bloody mess when you rip them apart, which you always do. I've got to stop this, you know?" He nodded, mouth covered. "I've got to stop being so willy-nilly."

I folded my arms. I remained still and calm. I was calm, I later realized, because I didn't believe Dan. I didn't believe that he thought our relationship was sloppy or haphazard, or that he wanted to split. When Dan finished talking, I stood up and shouldered the messenger bag on which I'd been sitting to keep my painters' pants clean. In those days I almost always wore white pants and a white T-shirt. Dan called it my marry-me garb.

"Okay. See you?" I said, too proud to argue my case.

Dan walked across the top of the park, through the palm trees, to his apartment on 20th Street. I walked down toward Mission High School and 18th Street, to my studio on Dorland. Once there, I pulled out the tomatoes, basil, mozzarella, and pasta—my solace in the kitchen when I still cooked. I set a pot of water on the stove to boil. Before it did, my phone rang.

"So," Dan said.

"So," I said.

"So, what are you doing for dinner?"

We ate together in my tiny kitchen, at my pine table with the turned green legs. I loved that apartment, the French doors on the closets, the jasmine in the backyard. Over our pasta Dan and I did not talk about the park. He just watched my face, as if it were a sunrise, and when we finished, he washed the dishes. With his back toward me, in his flannel shirt and faded jeans, he scrubbed so very slowly.

In Dan's lingering I realized he did not want to leave, and a year later he proposed: my apartment again, up on the roof, a dozen roses, his grandmother's ring. Given our jobs, for our wedding, we thought we'd write our own vows—express ourselves fully, marry in our own way. Then we attended the wedding of one of Dan's rock-climbing buddies, at which the betrothed promised to "love and belay." Next, a wedding at which the bride promised "to try to be faithful" while her groom promised "to relinquish control." Concerned that individuality and marriage vows didn't mix, we retreated to the wisdom of the ages, opting to make the standard pledges: to have and to hold, to love and to cherish, in sickness and in health, etc. In Olema, California, at the altar in the dappled sunshine, we were optimistic, cocky, and vague about the concept of marriage. We never discussed, nor did we consider discussing, *why* we were getting married nor what a good marriage, for us, would mean. It all seemed too obvious. I loved Dan, I loved how I felt with him. I wanted to be his wife.

During the first nine years of our marriage Dan and I just cruised, notching successes (house, kids), accumulating tensions (house, kids), thinking little about our expectations and not much more about our parents' marriages, both of which have lasted more than forty years. For two couples so demographically similar—all four of our parents are white, college educated, middle class, and born between 1936 and 1942; plus our mothers are now *friends,* as in they go to museums and out to lunch and discuss topics other than shared grandchildren—our folks set very different examples of how a marriage could be good.

Dan was raised by VW-bus-driving lefties so enthralled with each other that Dan sometimes felt left out. In their warm, simple Berkeley farmhouse on Virginia Street, catty-corner from a playground, each meal, each sunset was the most exquisite. In the evenings, Kit, Dan's mother, would squeeze Dan's father's gym-strong biceps. She'd throw back her head and laugh. Kit was a dashing young writer with a halogen smile. She was also the daughter of a self-made conservative San Francisco lawyer who'd never understood why his only daughter turned her back on country clubs and cashmere twin sets to spend her life with a criminal defense attorney, an Irish champion of the underdog who in 1964 clerked for the only black lawyer in southeast Georgia, cried during Satyajit Ray's "Apu Trilogy," and played banjo in the I'll Be Right Home, Honey Band. The answer to that riddle, of course, was romance. Romance mattered deeply in the Duane home. It made life magical, bearable, worthwhile. Kit passed this philosophy on to her children. When high school girls refused to talk to Dan, Kit told him they were just too intimidated by his good looks.

The lessons I learned about marriage and life from my parents' suburban redoubt could hardly have been more different. I never questioned their love, but from my seat—as a small child, at the end of our counter-height butcher-block dining table—marriage looked as if it were meant to be run like a small business, fueled by dependability, responsibility, and mutual respect. My parents, both Midwestern Jews, met on a blind date in New York City. My father, Doug, an earnest and Kennedy-loving real estate financier, then held season tickets to the Rangers. My mother, Judy, briefly married and divorced by age twenty-five, insisted she *loved* hockey and begged to attend all the games—that is, until she married my father at her own father's hotel in Omaha, Nebraska, after which she never set foot in a hockey stadium again. After my older sister was born, my parents followed my father's job from Manhattan to Indiana. Then, following the births of my brother and myself, they settled in Wellesley, the prototype community for *The Preppy Handbook,* a place where civic life was so tidy and shipshape that kids held bake sales at the town dump.

While romance reigned in Dan's childhood home, efficiency triumphed in mine. Thanks to my mother, beverage glasses left unattended for more than five minutes wound up in the dishwasher. Trash, too, including fireplace ashes, found its way into garbage barrels at an alarming rate—resulting in, on at least one occasion, the charbroiling of half the garage. Unless my steadier, slower-moving father tended the grill, steak was served rare, tuna was served rare, and chicken was served rare, too. On a typical day my mother woke at 7:15 a.m., left the house by 7:40 a.m., drove to Cambridge, worked eight hours as the personnel manager at Crimson Travel (company slogan, "Please, Go Away Soon!"), returned home (often with a speeding ticket), cooked a protein-starch-and-vegetable dinner, talked to her sisters or her mother, cleaned out some distant corner of the basement or garage, read a few pages of both the *New York Times* and the *Boston Globe,* acted shocked when my father declared it their "regular" bedtime, cleaned up all the stray shoes, books, and cups from the living room and kitchen, placed the day's newspapers in the recycling bin, walked upstairs, and fell asleep. This struck me as an excellent way to live. The only other married couple I observed at close range was the Zimbles, whom I idolized, partly because Mrs. Zimble was a graphic designer with great taste and Mr. Zimble, like my father, often fell asleep in the den watching TV or with a middlebrow book on his chest. Thus I grew up with this vision of love. One person is the rock, and the other runs around the rock, because that's how things worked with the married couples I knew. My father was the center of my mother's world, and my mother was always running around.

I loved my mother's energy, her optimism. I was clinging to her Levi's on Wellesley's Main Street long before I learned that attachment was the parenting holy grail. I even belted out the hokey songs she wrote on road trips (in hindsight, to brainwash us), including her crowning achievement, which I still sing to this day, "How happy we are! As we travel the land in our car!," set to the tune of "Home on the Range." By age eight I'd chosen to have my ponytails lopped off in favor of a pixie cut like hers. By age eleven I was talking on the phone while standing on my head (a pastime I do not continue but have imparted to my daughters), following my mother's belief that it was always better to do two things at once. (Three or more, however, looked risky. One night while cooking dinner, moderating a League of Women Voters teleconference, and doing laundry, my mother caught the phone cord on fire.) Still, I arranged my life as per my mother's example, rushing from class officer meetings, to student council meetings, to my after-school job as a student representative for the Department of Education all the while dating the steadfast and blessedly WASPy Andy Wilson, a boy as rock-like as my father in his sweetness and endless patience, and amused by my flitting around. The goal of all the rushing, at least in my family, was the security of effort, the buzz of accomplishment. Nobody talked about physical appearance or hedonic joys. These arenas were too subjective, too impervious to hard work. Pleasure took the form of good food at white-tablecloth restaurants. All conjugal affection took place out of sight. "You're a good doobie" was considered high praise.

Just before our wedding, with some money remaining from my boom-time civilian-spaceship book advance, Dan and I bought a run-down house on the edge of San Francisco. From the outside, it looked like a child's drawing, a green square with a blue door in the middle, upstairs and downstairs windows on either side. On the day we moved in, following a honeymoon at a borrowed beach cottage, we assumed that our big problems would be money and religion, as Dan is Christian, I'm Jewish. Neither turned out to be true. Over the years, we built, or more accurately, fell into a twenty-first-century companionate marriage. Only Dan and I were not just each other's lovers, economic partners (soon enough), coparents, and best friends. We were also each other's coworkers, editors, and primary readers. Both working from home, our lives resembled a C-list version of Joan Didion's and John Gregory Dunne's, whose days, according to Didion, "were filled with the sound of each other's voices." Except we had what I can only assume was a much more egregious lack of boundaries. We e-mailed each other many times a day, between our basement and attic offices. We also shared each other's flaws. Neither of us focused much on the future. Nobody made the girls practice piano or took the bags of old running shoes that accumulated in the closet to Goodwill. Had we been asked to pick two circles that best represented our marriage—choices ranging from wholly separate to almost entirely overlapping—we would have picked the most overlapping ones. According to psychology professor Arthur Aron, who along with his colleagues conducted a study based on these circles, this was ideal, predictive of the most satisfying marriage. But similarity produced problems. For instance, our lack of boundaries. We'd *both* lost steam 95 percent of the way through our DIY home remodel and as a result, two years after packing up the tools, we still had no master bathroom door.

3

What Is a Good Marriage?

How to start improving our marriage? What would "better" even look like? More happiness? Intimacy? Stability? Laughter? Fewer fights? All grievances resolved? A smoother partnership? More intriguing conversation? More excellent sex?

We all know or think we know what marriage is: a legal commitment between two people. The idea of the *good* marriage is ill-defined, not to mention anxiety-producing, as it forces all marrieds within earshot to ask themselves, Is *my* marriage good? Why do I think my marriage is good? How is my marriage not good? How does it let me down? In her 1995 book *The Good Marriage,* cowritten with Sandra Blakeslee, the psychologist Judith Wallerstein describes standing before a group of successful women "who had achieved success in our high-tech, competitive society and who appeared to have it all" and telling them she's interested in studying long-lasting marriages and what makes them "genuinely satisfying for both husband and wife."

She then asks, "Would any of you, along with your husbands, like to volunteer as participants in the study?"

The room explodes in laughter.

Dan was not immune to laughing at the good-marriage concept, either. In the weeks after I first broached the topic of marriage improvement, he'd lie on his side of the bed in the evening, reading Pavel Tsatsouline's *Power to the People! Russian Strength Training Secrets for Every American,* wondering what happened to his life. Dan's mother's advice on how to maintain a good marriage was to plan a yearly road trip on which you agree not to say anything more explosive on the first day than "Where's the map?" Mind you, Dan had no grounds for criticizing my let's-fix-it-*before*-it-breaks approach, as every few minutes he'd stand up from our platform bed to work on what he called "prehab," small exercises for the stabilizer muscles in his shoulders, hips, ankles, knees, and back, maneuvers that, in theory, would protect his body from getting hurt. He'd take a five-pound dumbbell and trace circles in the air around his head. Or he'd unfurl a yoga mat and crank out a few Jane Fonda–esque leg raises, to strengthen a tiny muscle called the gluteus medius, located near his ass.

I wanted to approach our marriage with the same care and vigor. The most common reason divorcing spouses cite for not seeking therapy is that they feel it's "too late." Still, my plan struck nearly everyone as wrong-headed and strange. Dan's two closest surf buddies extended their condolences. One slapped Dan on the back and said, "You poor bastard." The other said, "Dude, I think I know how this one ends."

Our improving began in the winter of 2009. During San Francisco's January rains, I started researching the standard marriage assessments, trying to understand how the experts parsed what made a marriage good.

The earliest one I found was written in 1933, just three years after Paul Popenoe founded the American Institute of Family Relations, the first marriage clinic in the United States. Popenoe, it turns out, was not interested in love or even in marriage. He was a eugenicist and the son of an avocado farmer, and after publishing a book about the date (as in, the fruit) crop and how to improve it, he turned his attention toward human beings, hoping to optimize the species and its procreative habits through twinned mechanisms: compulsory sterilization and marriage counseling. The sterilization he promoted for the feeble and crazy. (His book *Sterilization for Human Betterment* was translated into German by the Nazi government.) The marriage counseling he urged upon the not-so-feeble and not-so-crazy . . . and maybe not so brown-haired or brown-eyed, either. "If we [are] to promote a sound population," Popenoe reasoned, "we would not just have to get the right kind of people married, but we would have to keep them married."

The 1933 assessment worked on a system of merits and demerits, largely based on manners. Demerits for husbands included: "Picks teeth, nose, or sucks teeth in public." "Calls 'where is . . .' without first looking for object." "Teases wife about fatness, slowness, etc." Merits included: "Makes guests feel welcome; an interesting entertainer." "Well liked by men, courageous—not a sissy." "His children are pleased at his arrival home." The field of marriage assessment exploded in the wake of the IQ test developed during World War I. Choosing a mate based on desire, not demographics, was relatively new. The pseudo-scientific tests made the trend seem less impulsive and risky, both for individual couples and for society.

Still, I found even the more modern marriage assessment tests scattershot and beside the point. The Locke-Wallace Marital Adjustment Test, published in 1959, asked spouses to rank themselves along a continuum from "very unhappy" to "very happy." The Dyadic Adjustment Scale, published in 1976, focused on self-expression, querying, "How often do you and your mate 'get on each other's nerves'?" Others ranked relative agreement on matters ranging from recreation to in-laws. I was not alone in finding the tests suspect. Some psychologists at the University of Rochester likened the sloppy, unanalyzed history of marital assessments to conducting "research on fevers and fever medications

. . . . without knowing whether the thermometers were accurate to a single degree or +/- 10 degrees." More to the point, what did these tests aim even to tell us? "Am I happy?" Katha Pollitt asked in her takedown of America's happiness preoccupation. "What a stupid question."

Pollitt's point is that "happy" is such an inexact word. "Happy as in content? Joyful? Hopeful? Relieved? Counting my blessings? Intent on absorbing work?" That state also fluctuates broadly, in short intervals. Some days I felt exceedingly happy to be married to Dan. Others, I felt annoyed, envious of women not wed to men making pennies writing novels about ex-lovers. But I wasn't setting out to be the happiest wife. Nor did I need to know how my marriage ranked. I just wanted to find and protect all that was good in my marriage. I had a feeling there might be more. And when you start focusing on that, when you stop seeking grades (though for those of you who share my weakness for tests, here's the 2007 Couples Satisfaction Index*), you quickly realize that for all the endless talk about marriage—who should have the right to be in one, whether declining numbers of two-married-parent households are hurting America's children—we know surprisingly little about what makes a marriage good or how to keep one that way.

Even John Gottman, the patron saint of marriage research, already the dominant name in the field when Malcolm Gladwell came along and made him exponentially more famous as his prime example of snap judgments or "thin slicing" in *Blink,* knows a whole lot less about how to keep a marriage good than he or Gladwell would have us believe. In Gottman's so-called Love Lab, near Seattle, the psychologist promises

---

*   1. Please indicate the degree of happiness, all things considered, in your relationship. [Extremely unhappy to perfect, 0 to 6]
    2. I have a warm and comfortable relationship with my partner. [Not at all true to completely true, 0 to 5]
    3. How rewarding is your relationship with your partner? [Not at all to completely, 0 to 5]
    4. In general, how satisfied are you with your relationship? [Not at all to completely, 0 to 5]

he can analyze a five-minute conversation between two spouses and predict with 96 percent accuracy whether the couple will divorce over the course of fourteen years. Based on this, he sells vast numbers of books, DVDs, training for marriage counselors, workshops for couples, even weekend retreats with his own wife on Orcas Island, for which he charges four thousand dollars for two days and one night of semiprivate help. Yet many academics believe Gottman's claims are overblown, that he finds traits *correlated* with divorce but that he generates those correlations retrospectively, using videotaped interactions of married couples he knows have split. The result is that the link between divorce and what Gottman calls "Four Horsemen of the Apocalypse" (criticism, defensiveness, contempt, and stonewalling) is sort of like the link between earthquakes and radon gas. Radon levels often rise prior to earthquakes, but this does not mean the gas predicts the seismic activity. Almost always, when radon levels rise no earthquake follows. And so it is with Gottman's horsemen. Ninety-six percent of couples who divorce criticize, are defensive and contemptuous, and stonewall each other. But this does not make these behaviors accurate prophecies. It just makes them common.

Marriage researchers not selling marriage books, workshops, DVDs, or counseling admit to knowing surprisingly little. "We know you should hit less, hug more," one academic told me. "But that's like telling an obese person to eat less and move more. Everybody knows that."

So by necessity the design of my project would have to be organic. Dan and I would try what was available, see if it helped, feel our way forward without a map. This would lead to wrong turns and dead ends. But such is the state of marriage research. One scientist finds that people who smile in their high school yearbook photos stay married longer than people who don't; another determines that in the optimal husband-wife team the woman is five years younger and 27 percent smarter than the man. One determines that attachment is crucial between husbands and wives, just as it is between parents and children; another that satisfied couples view bad behavior as aberrant (he had a lousy day), not steady state (I married an ass). But a template for improving a marriage as a whole does not exist. In fact, Harry Reis, a professor at the University of Rochester, likens our current understanding of "relationship science" to the Buddhist parable of the Blind Men and the Elephant. One blind man "feels the tusk, inferring that elephants are hard and sharp-edged, like a blade. Another touches the soft, flexible ear, concluding that elephants are supple, resembling felt. A third imagines massive strength from grasping the pillarlike structure of the leg. The perspective of each is valid, as far as it goes. . . ." But no one, including us, has a marital theory of everything. No one understands the whole beast.

4
Self-Help

"What the fuck kind of name is Harville?" Dan barked defensively as I rooted in my nightstand for pens.

Harville Hendrix's Oprah-sanctioned self-help bestseller, *Getting the Love You Want,* was splayed on the bed between us. About three weeks had passed since I first mentioned to Dan the possibility of improving our marriage. During that time I'd read many marriage self-help books—figuring it might be best for us to start our marriage improvement alone together at home. Most of the books had titles like *How to Improve Your Marriage Without Talking About It* or *Twelve Hours to a Great Marriage,* titles that made me think marriage improvement was too hopeless and unpleasant to describe accurately at all. Mort Fertel's *Marriage Fitness* staked out the endpoint of the genre, in part because Fertel's personal story is so extreme and sad. He and his wife lost a newborn son, and then newborn twin daughters, all within two years. But even this, says Fertel, is not too dark a depth from which to save a marriage, nor is it cause for soul-searching or couples' therapy. Even in extremis, perhaps especially in extremis, one need only " 'make' love" (emphasis Fertel's) by setting aside one's problems and applying the laws of "marriage fitness." This process, as he describes it, is not wrenching or arduous. It's clean, technical, just a little systems upgrade, like bringing your Mac to the Genius Bar for an erase and reinstall.

That February the California poppies had begun bearing their tender orange heads in San Francisco's early spring. The blooms looked so vulnerable, so idiotically brave, rooted by the side of the road. I wanted to be that way, too, open and fearless. So I let Dan pick, from Hendrix, our first exercise—it only seemed sporting. I assumed he'd pick "positive flooding," a drill that involves listing all the nice things you wish your partner would say to you but never does, then sitting in a chair as that spouse walks circles around you, reading aloud from that list in an increasingly loud and emphatic voice. The instructions went a little far for my taste. By the end the circling spouse is supposed to be jumping "up and down, feet leaving the floor." I imagined Dan would pick this because he'd grown up in a family of epic praisers. (The most! The best ever! So gorgeous!) He craved compliments, and I was terrible at giving them. My parents tended to downplay and minimize. As a wife, I sided with the psychoanalyst Adam Phillips, believing that in marriage "the long applause becomes baffling."

But to kick off the project, Dan did not choose "positive flooding." He picked "re-romanticizing," another weakness of mine.

Our daughters, Hannah and Audrey, were sleeping upstairs: Hannah, eight and lanky, in her tidy room; Audrey, five and rowdy, in her messy one. Hannah and Audrey were so miraculous yet so exhausting, even now that after school they ran in the front door and out the back, to climb through the hole in our back fence and jump on our neighbor's trampoline. I'd recently asked my cousin, two years into marriage and two months into fatherhood, how being a parent was treating him. He and his wife had been using a sleep training approach that involved bouncing their daughter atop a huge Swiss ball while saying "Sssshhh! Sssshhh! Sssshhh!," the shushing in rhythm with the hops. This hadn't been working. My cousin looked chalky, wasted, and grim. "My daughter is like a dying star," he told me with zero affect. "All the energy of the universe is being sucked toward her."

Dan and I had left that phase, thank god. But still I worried about our daughters' disruptive powers, especially right now, as Dan was fuming, doing that thing he often does, excessively airing his feelings—in this case, stating at volume that Hendrix's book was written for "emotional retards"—hoping an adequate venting of his emotions would make them disappear, or at least take up residence in me. My specific concern at that moment was that his booming, embattled self-expression would wake the girls, sending them in their nightgowns to the top of the stairs, scuttling our marriage-improvement efforts for the night. Dan seemed oblivious to this, though at some level it was his intent. He picked up the Hendrix and tossed it to the floor. "We don't need that stupid thing," he said, trying a different tack—flirting—pulling me toward him, creating a clever catch-22: How could I think I was improving my marriage while rebuffing sex?

I should mention that at this point neither Dan nor I had spent much time considering the downside of improvement: the fact that improving requires deliberate change, and that change demands a person identify an area of interest, acknowledge an imperfection, however implicit or slight. Normally, I'm comfortable as a critic. I'm from the East Coast and Jewish, not averse to finding flaws. Then I moved to California and with alarming frequency people began describing me as "real."

I didn't know what "real" meant at first or if it was intended as a compliment or a slight. Even Dan used the word—for the first time at Baker Beach, a miraculous beach, the *most* beautiful beach, as the Duanes would say, right by the Golden Gate Bridge. During a party there, Dan strummed Neil Young's "The Needle and the Damage Done" on his guitar and played two-man volleyball. Meanwhile, I grew inward and anxious on my towel. I didn't play guitar, I couldn't set or spike, and

I made a lousy cheerleader. So I laced up my running shoes (which I often carry with me in case of social panic) and ran along the Land's End trail toward the Cliff House, returning just as Dan and my Grotto office mates were folding the net.

"You can't fake it, can you?" Dan said, squinting into the sun as we walked toward his blue pickup.

"What?"

"You can't fake it. You're just so real."

I'd heard this a few times already, mostly from women. For a while I took it as a backhanded compliment for my as-yet-unwaxed brow line and unhighlighted brown hair. But then I realized the problem was, and is, much deeper, stemming from an innate literalness, a lack of cool, a feeling (accompanied by an unguarded look in my eyes) that if you discuss getting together for coffee sometime you should follow up the next day to set a date. In our earliest days Dan and I often discussed the concept of "cool." He loved it; I had misgivings. I fooled no one about the true coordinates of my native habitat, least of all my future husband. He had the ear and drifty-seeming soul of a poet. My ear and soul, I'm sorry to report, have always seemed best suited to a debate team.

Re-romanticizing, Step 1: Complete the following sentence as many ways as possible: "I feel loved and cared about when you . . ."

Dan quickly jotted down *submit to kissing, clean the kitchen, tell me I look studly. . . .*

"Let's try for ten," I said, remembering a conversation I'd had earlier that week with the director of the California Healthy Marriage Initiative. I'd called the organization in the vain hope of creating a detailed map of the marriage interventions that would be best for us. The director had asked me to rate my marriage on a scale of one to ten.

"Ten," I said.

I could tell in his silence that he thought I was deluded.

"And what would your husband rate your marriage?" he asked, pressing.

I said "ten" again.

I meant this at the time—though I do see the director's point: Who with a perfect marriage calls seeking marriage help? Proving him right, that first night of marriage betterment, on our queen-sized platform bed, I had a hard time thinking of ten things Dan did that made me feel loved.

Dan suffered from the same problem. "Ten?! I can't even think of three."

In *Intimate Terrorism,* the psychologist Michael Vincent Miller describes marriage darkly as "mocking" our "fondest dreams," arguing that the institution is not the wellspring of love we imagine it to be. Instead, it's a "barbaric competition over whose needs get met"; it's "two people trying to make a go of it on the emotional and psychological supplies that are only sufficient to one."

Until reading this I'd never thought of Dan as my adversary. I'd never even viewed my marriage as a negotiation, though of course, in some ways, it was. We had bartered often early in our marriage, even during our engagement, as nearly everything in our lives together was still up for grabs. Where would we live? How much money was enough? Who would cook dinner or watch the baby, and who would go to the gym?

From the very beginning—starting with that night in 1998 when Dan broke up with me, then washed the dishes slowly in my apartment, making it clear he wanted to stay—I had no game. I loved Dan. I wanted to reinvent myself for him, and as a result I lost our first major bargaining session badly. This was a year and a half later, in the fall of 1999. We'd traveled to Wellesley to see my parents, who hadn't yet moved to

California. They still lived in the fifties modern ranch house I'd grown up in, on quiet Cartwright Road, just across the street from Beebe Meadow, through which ran the skunk cabbage– and cattail-laden Fuller Brook.

As an adult, I had never really known what to do with myself in my parents' home. I suppose I still felt off-balance from the tautological mantra my folks had employed against unoccupied and complaining children: "Only boring people get bored." I loved my parents and craved being with them, but I couldn't sleep in Wellesley. I couldn't relax, and I really didn't know what to do among their pastel tweed sofas with six-foot-two-inch, redheaded, surf- and mountain-loving Dan.

As a kid I'd escaped to Beebe Meadow, and when I lost interest in the cattails and skunk cabbage, I walked down to Debbie Zimble's house, where they had a go-cart and VCR. But the small meadow yielded its wonders too quickly to enchant an adult, and the Zimbles had divorced and moved. So Dan and I spent our afternoons walking along the Charles River, in Cambridge. The weather was perfect, the air still crisp, the grass still green. I'd lived there, in Cambridge, near Central Square, in my early twenties, sharing an apartment in a lopsided triple-decker with my brother, David, who'd just finished Harvard Business School. David was good with money in the second-nature way some kids are good with pets. He didn't write for the high school newspaper, he sold ads for it, shocking the nice bearded faculty adviser when he returned from Wellesley's ice cream and pizza parlors with several thousand dollars the paper didn't need. By the time I shared the flat with my brother, he'd begun amassing his inevitable investment banker's fortune. I worked in a café, wrote quizzes for *YM* magazine, and ran along the Charles River, timing my pace from bridge to bridge, feeling an enormous sense of accomplishment, yet making little of my life.

I knew Boston was too stodgy to interest Dan and Wellesley too suburban. But Cambridge? I loved it there. I assumed Dan would love it, too. So I spelled out my vision: At some point we'd move back here, maybe to Somerville. Dan would walk along the river in some old Patagonia fleece he'd worn climbing El Capitan, feeling proud of the youth he'd spent in the West, devoted to ambitions of the body, yet thrilled to be here now, in the East with me, pursuing the life of the mind.

Dan did not agree. Just as I felt hopelessly like a transplant in California, Dan believed that he possessed a need or deficiency that made him permanently unadaptable to life outside the West. He took his bearings from the mountains and ocean. He'd loved studying with grouchy A. R. Ammons (a master nature poet) during his four years at Cornell. But Dan hated the East Coast geography, its sameness. To him, every hill looked like every other hill, and behind it, depressingly, more copies. The afternoon of his last Cornell exam, he flew back to California for good. Walking along the Charles with me, ten years later, Dan told me my East Coast fantasy was not going to happen. Ever.

"I could never be happy here," he said that day in 1999, his feet crackling the dry leaves.

"Really?" I said. "I know that Wellesley is horrible, and Boston is horrible. But not even here?"

Dan held his eyes steady and clasped my hands. "This could never feel like home."

Home. Wasn't home a state of mind? Something we'd build in each other? Weren't homes things created through boxes moved, beds made and remade, decisions to keep one's chin up? That's how it had always been in my family—great-grandparents emigrating from Eastern Europe, settling in the Midwest, children dispersing for jobs and love. Home was where you paid the mortgage and sent the kids to school. Why Dan's stalwart commitment to place? Was California more important to him than I was?

That day I didn't ask. I didn't want to know.

I didn't enjoy this haggling and neither did Dan, but at the beginning we didn't see an alternative. So much had to be decided. We stayed in California, bought a house. But now—a decade after the Charles walk, two decades after Dan had graduated from college—our lives had settled. Dan cooked and grocery shopped. I cleaned and tended finances. We'd found a routine with each other, stopped seeking concessions, and our marriage felt better for it. Yet with *Getting the Love You Want* splayed on our duvet, the competitive mind-set came roaring back, as I reasoned, subconsciously anyway, that any changes we made in our relationship would either be toward Dan's vision of marriage and away from mine or the other way around. Admitting too much satisfaction seemed tantamount to ceding the upper hand. So I held my ground.

I, too, failed to think of ten things Dan did that made me feel loved.

"Okay," I said, "let's quit after eight."

Step 2

Recall the romantic stage of your relationship. . . . Complete this sentence: *I used to feel loved and cared about when you . . .*

Dan, head propped on two pillows, drew on his paper one of those circles with a line through it, symbolizing, he told me, "the null set." (He later insists he meant that there was nothing I'd *stopped* doing that had made him feel loved and cared for, but let's just say this was unclear at the time.) Then he grabbed my list.

"Looked giddy to come through the door and see me," Dan said, groaning. "Are you kidding me? You don't even notice my existence when you come home. It's like you're blind and deaf to everyone but the kids."

Dan was exaggerating, joking, sort of. I thought I'd avoided becoming one of those mothers who transferred all of her romantic energy from her husband to her children. Or at least I thought I'd *ceased* being one of those mothers once Audrey stopped nursing and I had my body back to myself. Apparently I'd failed. Yet Dan, in my estimation, hadn't mastered the parent-spouse balance, either. Yes, I harbored a (to Dan's mind) bad habit of running—literally running—back to the house if I'd been gone from the girls too long. But Dan often competed with them for my attention.

"Do you actually think a two-hundred-pound man who works at

home with his wife needs to fight with his children over their mother's attention in the forty-five minutes those children have before leaving for school?" I shot back in response to Dan's crack about looking giddy when I walked through the door.

Dan countered, "Would it be so hard to acknowledge Hannah, Audrey, *and* me?"

Well.

I knew people so afraid of being alone they made themselves impossible to be with. I knew parents so fearful of their children becoming sick they never allowed their babies to build strong immune systems by fighting off germs. Was I manufacturing my own worst nightmare—so determined to improve my marriage I would cause it to implode? Maybe. Dan's surf buddies and the women who laughed at Wallerstein's question about "good marriage" already understood something I had only just learned: that poking at a good marriage would rouse the sleeping dogs, the dormant irritations. *Well, honey, if you really want to know, I hate that Aveda face cream you buy me for Christmas every year, and you snore.* In the short term, at least, this does not constitute improvement. It only undermines your confidence, making everything worse.

Had I been wrong to think my marriage was good? Had I misunderstood the physics? I had always thought of my good marriage as floating atop a sea of goodness, perhaps adrift at times, but essentially stable when pushed. But what if my good marriage was instead teetering on a precipice of goodness and in my fear of stasis I'd cause it to topple down? Much of the commentary I'd read on modern marriage was terrifying. Michael Miller, for instance, described "the marital ghetto"—*the marital ghetto?*—as "the human equivalent of a balanced aquarium, where the fish and the plants live indefinitely off each other's waste products": marriage not just as a refuge, a cocoon for the tired and risk-averse, but marriage as a self-enforced prison in which two deluded cowards subsist on each other's shit.

Perhaps the reason we'd been striving in child-raising but not in marriage is that parenting is a dictatorship and marriage is a democracy. In parenthood there's no presumption that good means equal. There's zero illusion of fairness. The children do not vote on the bylaws. There's no charade of coming to consensus, no debate over which discipline philosophy the whole family likes best. But with a spouse, particularly a contemporary American companionate spouse, equality is foundational, assumed. Yes, I'd lost the first round of negotiations with Dan, concerning East Coast or West. I'd started in the unrecoverable bargaining position of already living in California and being the first to fall in love. But by now, in what might be called our middle child-rearing years, the scales had balanced, possibly even tipped in my favor. A friend had recently told me he thought I was the boss in my marriage. Did I really want to upend my relationship, examine every aspect, negotiate it anew?

The question soon became moot because there in our bedroom, with its adjoining doorless bathroom, our re-romanticizing fizzled.

Step 3
Think of some loving and caring behaviors that you have always wanted but never asked for. Complete this sentence: *I would like you to . . .*
Step 4
Combine your lists. Rank all the behaviors on a scale of one to five, one being the most important.
Step 5
Trade lists.

On Dan's paper I saw a huge black "1" next to *give me backrubs EVER, and give them like you enjoy it.* He put a "4" next to *hug me from behind.*

"And what do you mean by this?" he said, reading aloud from my paper, loudly grinding our progress to a halt. "*Ask me what I want to eat?*

Are you talking about breakfast? Because breakfast is okay. I don't mind giving you a choice for breakfast, but dinner's tough. . . ."

The food situation in our house was a little extreme. More on that later. Dan retreated to the bathroom and started brushing his teeth. "Do you really think this project is a good idea?" he asked when he finished.

In that moment I realized my favorite books about marriage—Calvin Trillin's *About Alice* and Joan Didion's *The Year of Magical Thinking*—included one spouse who was dead.

5
Therapy

In March, the cherry trees blooming, their pink tear-shaped petals scattering in the wind, Dan and I drove across San Francisco to the upscale Laurel Village neighborhood for our first couples' therapy session. En route we discussed not shaking the bushes of our union too hard.

Dan had just flown home from London, where he'd been reporting a story on his hero, Fergus Henderson, a chef who defines a pig's head as "a romantic dinner for two." Henderson suffers from Parkinson's but told Dan he'd stopped reading about the disease because, as he put it, "The more I know, the more symptoms I have." Following suit, we'd thought it best with our new therapist to dissect only the good parts of our relationship, given that marriage—and as we were learning, marriage improvement—can bring out people's worst. Even those who are generally tolerant, wise, patient, and giving are often short and rude to their mates. I'd once heard about a woman, a friend of a friend, who had tried to fix her marriage by treating her husband like someone she did not know. I'd also winced at the opening of Anton Chekhov's story "The Lady with the Dog." The narrator describes the protagonist's wife as "a tall, erect woman with dark eyebrows, staid and dignified." Then he gives us her husband's less charitable view: "He secretly considered her unintelligent, narrow, inelegant, was afraid of her, and did not like to be at home."

How much did we really want to share?

Earlier I'd asked my friend Emily, a psychiatrist, to help me assemble a list of therapists for me and Dan to try. Emily grew up in Newton, the town right next to Wellesley, and she's smart and warm and funny—one of my favorite people on earth. Together we decided Dan and I should sample couples' counseling, group workshops, sex therapy, and cognitive behavioral therapy, starting with Holly Gordon, an analyst Emily described as excellent and intense. I called, explained our project (including the fact that I intended to write about it), and booked us an appointment.

Dan and I had never before seen a psychologist together. The American Association for Marriage and Family Therapists claims that its members are treating 1.8 million people at any given time. Marriage therapy is the default intervention for couples, the dutiful course of action, though personally I was wary. I'd long favored, instead, the fake-it-'til-you-make-it approach to life. Why turn over the rocks of one's history just to see what's underneath? Relative to marriage, this fear made particular sense to me, as the couples' therapy carries not only the standard threat of learning things about one's self one might prefer not to know, but also bears the double hazards of saying things to one's spouse—and hearing things from that spouse—that are better left unsaid. Even some marriage counselors are outwardly critical of their peers; among them, William J. Doherty, director of the Marriage and Family Therapy program at the University of Minnesota, who worries that "inept and individualistic marriage therapists" have undermined the field. In his book *Take Back Your Marriage,* he writes, "If you talk to a therapist in the United States about problems in your marriage, I believe that you stand a good risk of harming your marriage." He then defines the phenomenon of "therapist-induced marital suicide," citing four root causes. The first is the natural tendency of mental health professionals to find mental health problems. ("I'm afraid you're married to a narcissistic personality disorder." Who's going to stick around for that?) The second is rampant incompetence in the field. (The American Association of Marriage and Family Therapists does not require any specialized training for a therapist to treat couples, and as a result, many therapists can't help their clients and thus deliver the message that their union is doomed.) The third is overt undermining ("If you're not happy in your marriage, why do you stay?"), and the fourth is the therapist's supposed neutrality, a stance that tends to reinforce the position of the spouse with a foot out the door. ("Imagine if a parent came in and said, 'I've had it with this teenager, I want to get him into foster care,' and the therapist said, 'Well, OK. Let's help you get the kid out of the house.'") In November 1995 *Consumer Reports* published an article titled "Does Therapy Help?" Satisfaction with marriage counselors was lower than with psychiatrists, psychologists, and social workers. Only 37 percent of consumers felt helped by marriage therapists "to some degree."

I punched in the door code to Holly's office, my fingers shaking. Her block housed Honeys & Heroes, a children's boutique selling tiny Rock & Republic jeans, undersized Michael Kors shoes. I felt poor and underdressed. Dan, meanwhile, stood steadily by my side, his palm heavy on my shoulder, his breathing even. Dan liked shrinks and shrinks liked him. When we met, he was seeing a therapist to help him work through "the bad lady," as we called his previous girlfriend. Then, four years into our marriage, he returned to therapy and started taking antidepressants to deal with his grief from a pregnancy we'd lost. If not for the expense, he might well have continued. He enjoyed sifting through his feelings, depth-sounding for answers. He was very articulate. Emotions hit him hard.

But I was skeptical of therapy, or at least very well defended. I'd seen a clutch of psychologists in my late teens when I'd been anorexic, a fact that still embarrassed me partly because it seemed so expected for an overachieving girl from a food-focused family. Between my seventeenth and eighteenth birthdays, at five feet eight inches, I dropped below ninety pounds. This billboarding of my mental health had led me to six weeks at Hahnemann Hospital's in-patient psychiatric ward, the first week on a feeding tube, the others eating. Yet I refused to take in much knowledge about myself. I rationalized, during therapy, that I was smarter and more powerful than the psychologists. I, not they, knew the facts of my life, right? I withheld or meted out information, so how could they know more about my situation than I? This was childish, but even once I admitted that, I didn't embrace therapy. Still I'd brought us here, now, to examine our marriage. Why? Did I think intense Holly might say, "You two are doing great! Go home!" and give me a gold star?

Holly Gordon, when she retrieved us from the waiting room, appeared straight out of studio casting—rail thin, short hair, eyes like one-way valves. She immediately dismissed our plan to stick with discussing the good parts of our marriage and leaving the rest unsaid.

"To get the most out of your time here we need to talk about some dissatisfaction or problem, something you're trying to improve." She closed a double set of soundproofed doors behind her. She then lowered herself into a reclining nylon lawn chair in front of her chaise longue, explaining, "Please excuse my posture. I've injured my back."

The rest of her room was more conventional—a few windows, a bookcase, scattered clocks, Japanese-inspired prints. Dan and I settled into matching blue club chairs a couple of feet apart. I reached a hand over to him. I felt very proud of my husband, here, under minor duress. I thought Holly might want to note that.

"Do you want me to start?" I asked Dan.

"Yeah. Go ahead."

I turned to face Holly. "So, Dan gets very involved in his hobbies."

39

"I have obsessions," Dan said.

"Dan has obsessions." As evidence, I told Holly about the time Dan came to the hospital, in 2002, to visit me and four-pound premature Hannah, and all he could talk about was the San Francisco building code. A week prior, to vent the anxiety of imminent fatherhood, Dan had torn the front steps off our house. This seemed fine: We had five weeks until my due date. Hannah was then born four weeks early, the skinniest, scrawniest baby either of us had ever seen. Of course Dan adored her, holding her up to the vast sealed windows, pointing west toward the beach, east toward the Sierras, introducing her to his beloved natural world. But he was also petrified of giving his heart to this ethereal creature, then watching her disappear. Hannah was almost weightless. Swaddled, she reached halfway up Dan's forearm. Dick, Dan's father, described her as still "on the other side."

That first week Hannah remained in the NICU, and I slept in the hospital, too, so that I could nurse. Afternoons Dan visited, bearing rattles and plush toys for Hannah and barbecued chicken from the Bi-Rite Market for me. I'd try to tell him about our reality (*our* now meaning Hannah's and mine): how she'd fall asleep too quickly while suckling, the heart murmur the doctors felt confident would go away. Dan, alone in our house, inhabited a separate and parallel universe. He'd lost a wife and gained a puny, terrifying baby. His mind darted away, as it so often did, from anxiety into obsession, away from our premature infant and toward the far more concrete and less scary problem of our house's old front stairs: how to rebuild them, how to calculate their rise and run.

One evening Dan and I actually left the hospital and drove a few blocks down to Fillmore Street for dinner.

"God, it's so weird," I said over my pasta, worried for the first of what would be many times that I was betraying Hannah by being out with Dan. "I haven't been off the maternity ward in five straight days. I feel like I've been living in one of those biosphere domes."

"Hey, do you think an average rise of eight and three-quarters inches would feel too steep?"

"And I just feel so guilty, like somehow Hannah's being in the NICU is my fault."

"Because I could do eight and a half, but then I'd have to rebuild the mid-flight landing."

Seven years later, back in Holly's office, our therapist folded her bony hands across her reclined chest. "You're insulated," she said to Dan.

Insulated. We both paused at the aptness of her word.

"Yes," Dan finally said. "Absolutely. If Liz could have reached inside, actually broken through and said, 'Honey, what's really going on?,' I would have just disintegrated in fear."

When it was Dan's turn to gripe for Holly's benefit, he outlined my distaste for French kissing—it made me feel claustrophobic—and our problem with praise. These were real issues between us, but also tales many-times-told. We gravitated toward them, I think, because we did not want Holly to control the story. We did not want to commit "therapist-induced marital suicide." We did not want to become like John Updike's Maples, Joan saying to Richard nine years into their marriage, in a story called "Giving Blood," "I asked you not to talk. . . . Now you've said things I'll never forget." We did not want to use therapy to set a pick for our divorce.

So in lieu of mining our history for newer and harsher truths, Dan and I pursued the lesser offense of making the other sound crazy. I must say, I assumed I'd have the upper hand as Dan, everyone knew, was the nutty one in our marriage. He was quicker to anger, more flagrantly emotional. He was the one with the road rage problem. The one taking antidepressants. The one with all the obsessions. The one who came unglued.

This viewpoint had solidified in 2004, when Hannah was a toddler, during a stretch in which Dan spent an eccentric amount of time in our basement, considering where to place the tie-down bolts, certain the foundation was going to cave. For those of you who don't live in earthquake territory, tie-down bolts are huge pieces of steel that you drill through your house's sill plate, down into the concrete, so that when the earth shakes, your life savings do not fall off their footings and crack. The bolts are big and ugly, and installing them is grueling work. But it was not the pulse of the roto-hammer that was undermining Dan, nor the fact that when he stood up straight his six-foot-two-inch frame became veined with cobwebs. That year, we'd come off a horrible spring. Dan had agreed we could have another baby. Then, in March, we lost that baby. Or at least that's what we called it, *lost*. The verb was a lie. We ended the pregnancy, by choice, more than halfway through the term.

Hannah was then a year and a half old, bald as an egg and only twenty pounds. But she spoke in sentences, like a preschooler, and as a result, when she chattered in public, which she often did from the high perch of her kid-carrier backpack, people stared at her like a singing cat. Dan and I were maturing at a less impressive rate. He'd completed his novel but my savings were drying up. I worked hard as a journalist, but even back then, before journalism started its death rattle, the checks couldn't accumulate fast enough. Adding pressure: I wanted another baby, badly, and we couldn't afford one in our present life. The schedule we'd devised to care for Hannah—Dan would work 6:00 a.m. to noon; I'd work noon to 6:00 p.m.; no nanny fees; just as productive as we were before—had turned out to be pure fantasy. We shared the cost of a nanny with a friend. We squeaked by; no way could we afford child care for two.

Should Dan quit writing and become a building contractor? Should we sell our house? Weekends we'd buckle Hannah, whom we still called Tiny, into her leopard-print car seat to visit open houses in outlying towns, searching for the solution to the ten-dimensional puzzle that was our life: We needed a cheaper place to live but one still close to our families, a community in which we might make some friends, where Dan could still surf. Half Moon Bay? Felton? Sebastapol? Sunday evenings we'd roll back home, feeling defeated and trapped. Given the rent check we drew off our in-law unit, moving to a house with no rental in a marginally cheaper town wasn't going to help much. Desperate to do something—to feel the rush of a problem solved—I repainted our bedroom blue and bought a new striped, vaguely beachy cotton rug. But while the gestures were cheering for a week or two, they were also cosmetic and cheap. What I really wanted was not to worry about money and to live in a home with a place to hang my clothes. Our bedroom had one small closet, but I'd ceded it to Dan. He claimed that if putting away his clothes was at all difficult, his shirts and jeans would remain in heaps on the floor. I resisted this for several years, then gave in, sick of the heaps. He was right.

One night after putting Hannah down in her crib I told Dan my new mantra: "Whole life creative act."

"What?" he said, closing the bedroom door behind him. You needed to close the door to walk around the end of the bed, as the mattress filled up most of the room.

"Whole life creative act," I repeated. "I think that should be our new working concept. We need to conceive of our lives in terms of *all* the things we want to create, not just our work."

Dan sat down on the white brocade coverlet we'd received as a wedding gift. It was so delicate and lovely, and for this reason I'd left it in its box for almost four years. But a few months prior I'd pulled it out. This was not a practice life. What was I waiting for? A dirt-free period? The coverlet was already stained.

I sensed Dan's eyes softening, his watery blue irises thawing from crystalline to warm. This was a very Berkeley concept I was proposing, that worth, particularly self-worth, should not be shackled to work.

"Whole life creative act, huh?" Dan said, lying flat, staring at the ornate medallion under the light fixture on the ceiling, resting his big red head near my hips.

"Yes, that's totally it," I said. "The whole point is to have a good life, right? That's what we want together. Who cares that you can string together one perfect sentence after another if you're so miserable with anxiety you can't embrace the world."

Dan kept staring at the medallion, rubbing the three-day whiskers under his chin, trying to figure out if I was playing a rhetorical trick, attempting to gain something for myself that was bad for him.

I repeated the mantra the following night: *whole life creative act.* Dan stared at the ceiling again. "No, really," I said. "I think it's a really great concept for us—not to get too focused on a single route to happiness. You know that part I love of *Siddhartha,* when he realizes he can find enlightenment not just listening to the river but listening to anything? We need that—to let go of the idea that there's one path to happiness. Especially if we're on a path that doesn't really lead to happiness anyway."

Dan rubbed his chin, still unshaven, and pursed his lips.

Whole life creative act, whole life creative act. It took me a few weeks and many dozens of repetitions of the mantra, but Dan came around. He agreed to put aside his literary writing and work at earning money, an enterprise that he suspected (correctly, it turned out) would bring him more satisfaction than he'd permitted himself to believe.

This meant we could try to have a second baby. I was overjoyed.

So five months later and nearly as pregnant, Dan and I crossed town together, to the Kaiser hospital, for my twenty-week sonogram, the one where they tell you if you're having a boy or a girl and measure all the fetal parts to make sure everything's on track. I pulled my shirt up over my belly, which was swollen but not huge, as if inflated by a bike pump. During the scan the technician informed us that the baby was a boy (prompting Dan to rush out into the hall and call his father: "Start organizing the rock climbing gear!"). The technician also, after Dan returned, said that he was "having a hard time" capturing images of the baby's intestines, but I was then such a medical naïf I didn't understand the code. I didn't know that any mention of an anomaly, even a technical one, is cause for concern, as the tech performing the scan cannot comment on the status of the fetus; he can only comment on the test. So I wiped the conductive jelly off my stomach, wriggled into my pants, and hustled with Dan to the car. I was tired—exhausted, as I had been for weeks—but I had a plane to catch. I was flying to Houston to report a story on parents who go to heroic lengths for children with rare genetic diseases.

Three days later, awaiting my flight home, my cell phone rang: Kaiser. Can you come back?

The follow-up sonogram revealed bonelike spots in the fetal bowel. Also, anomalies in the kidney and brain. The doctor who explained this said he was very sorry, and then he sent me stumbling up Geary Street, to the dilapidated genetics-counseling office. There, a woman with button-front gabardine pants who could not have been more than twenty-five years old escorted me into an office filled with spider plants and asked me a battery of questions so she could complete a genetic family tree. Are your maternal grandparents living? How did they die? What about your paternal grandparents? How did they die? Your parents? Any major diseases? What about your parents' siblings? Any cancer there?

Dan was home, writing a magazine story. We'd never discussed his joining me that day. I'd gone to all of Hannah's prenatal checkups alone, and that suited me fine. Now the young counselor with the gabardine pants asked me about Dan's family. His parents, his grandparents, his aunts, his uncles . . . a whole litany of awful, deathly questions. I felt relieved that Dan had not come. Our baby did not have cancer. I did not have cancer. Did we really need to discuss this now? Dan would have exploded with rage.

I sat unmoving, tears streaming, staring at the spider plants as this counselor with button-front pants explained the fetus most likely had some kind of chromosomal abnormality, maybe a trisomy like Down, or else the fetus had a congenital infection. The following day, a doctor with a very long needle pulled some murky amniotic fluid from my belly. Results from the amniocentesis would be available within two weeks—at which point we could decide whether we wanted to continue with the pregnancy or not.

That two-week gap was horrible. I was pregnant—visibly so, I could feel kicks—but I no longer felt sure I was having a baby. Dan and I, nauseated with fear, had agreed that we wouldn't continue a pregnancy that would lead to a gravely ill child, though we hadn't forced ourselves to define "gravely ill" yet. Nothing made sense. One afternoon, hoping to blunt my misery for a few minutes, I drove to Hayes Valley, to my favorite clothing store, to buy myself a shirt. I thumbed the racks, sorted by color. Then I froze. What size did I want? My size now? A bigger size for later in pregnancy? My pre-pregnancy size, in which to pretend I was normal once we destroyed the baby I was carrying the following week?

I stumbled to the car, sure I shouldn't be driving yet desperate to be back home, to not see in the eyes of strangers my swollen belly, falsely advertising joy and hope. Once in our house I closed my eyes and waited until 6 p.m.—the time, during that wait for the amnio results, when the native New Englander in me allowed for a dose of Valium.

When the genetics counselor called to inform me I had contracted cytomegalovirus, or CMV, I was running the water for Hannah's bath. Dan was out interviewing a subject for an article. In hindsight, I don't understand why the counselor told me anything when Dan was not home, but I can still hear her voice: light as a child's, unbroken by the reverb of personal loss. In this galling timbre she explained that even with the diagnosis of CMV nobody could tell us for sure what this meant regarding the health of our unborn baby. All that was certain was that if a woman contracts CMV for the first time while she's in her second trimester of pregnancy, and if the virus is passed to the fetus—which in my case it had been, given the spots in the bowel, kidney, and brain—the consequences can be dire. Our baby would most likely be deaf, perhaps also visually impaired, and almost certainly very mentally retarded.

I clutched Hannah, clung to her perfect skin. She still had a tiny crease, a line down the center of the bulb of her nose, a small seam that reminded me that she was something we made; she did not emerge fully formed. Above her nose were Dan's eyes, clear blue, and to my amazement, I hadn't freaked her out and made her start crying yet. Methodically, I pulled off her clothes and as I washed her I focused on moving my hands in the way she expected—washcloth to her tummy, rubber ducks to the lip of the tub, thumb to index finger to flick the ducks, creating those small splashes that made her laugh. While Hannah soaked, and hopefully kept calm, I called Dan, asked him to come home. When he arrived I repeated the nightmarish vagaries—the virus, the deafness, the very probable but not absolute mental impairment, the maddening lack of certainty.

Dan sat down on the bare wood floor just where he'd been standing. "But we can do something to save our son, right?" he said, shaking. "We can help him—our son. He's our son."

I slunk down next to him, holding Hannah in her hooded towel.

"Are you even sure he's that sick?" Dan asked, his whole body convulsing.

I said no.

The next day a friend—a doctor—dropped off a packet of research papers. I'd called her late the night before, hoping for firmer answers. Our house already felt empty, drained.

"I'm so sorry," she said when I opened the door. "I searched the literature. I so dearly wish I was coming here with better news." The packet, she explained, was thick but not very useful. No good studies existed, as almost all the CMV subjects in them had ended their pregnancies before reaching term.

We sat, this friend and I, together on our front steps, the steps Dan had built once Hannah and I were back in the house. We watched the cars roll down Ellsworth Street. Everybody seemed to be driving too fast.

"Do you know what you're going to do?" my friend asked.

I closed my eyes.

"You know this prognosis could make a child with Down syndrome look like a walk in the park?"

She left. I closed the door, clutching the packet of useless papers.

We agonized but we did not waver. Both Dan's parents and mine urged us to think about Hannah. They counseled that there was no shame in trying again. Dan and I did not speak much. Words sounded tinny and flat. How could I say that I knew I could love this son but I also feared we'd all drown in his needs, that we'd lose ourselves, each other, and Hannah in the darkness? I felt cowardly, overwhelmed, heartbroken, and small.

"I'm not strong enough," I said to Dan.

He held me and cried.

We decided to abort.

Dan and I were together on this, in the sense that we did not disagree. But while I disintegrated, Dan walled himself off from his own feelings. He kept our life running. He made Hannah feel safe. He wrote my articles. He held my monstrous body at night. Making matters worse, while Kaiser supported our decision, even subtly encouraged it (what were the tests for, really, if not to give us the option to abort?), no one in San Francisco would do the procedure. We were told if we wanted to get rid of the baby—and please, hurry before he's viable—we needed to drive an hour north, to another Kaiser hospital, in Santa Rosa. There a doctor with waist-length hair and a self-satisfied I-feel-your-pain style inserted seven straws of dried seaweed into my cervix to dilate it. He instructed us to return the following day.

While Hannah spent the evening with Dan's parents, Kit and Dick,

Dan and I drove to a hotel in Bodega, on the coast. We hoped natural beauty might help. It didn't. Nothing mattered. I pulled inward and waited. In the morning we returned to the hospital, along the same winding road. Our life was running backward, like a film projector, jamming. Before the surgery I threw up the antinausea medication. I woke to cold tears on my face.

For a few groggy hours I felt ecstatic not to be pregnant, as I'd felt queasy nearly the whole time. Then I spent the remainder of the spring misshapen and disoriented, unmoored by the milk seeping from my breasts but no baby, lost in a blur of sadness and work. Dan, meanwhile, fixated on our house's foundation: It seemed so old and flaky. One week he invited three cement experts to drop by. All, despite self-interest, vouched for our foundation's soundness. Still Dan couldn't believe them. For weeks he remained downstairs, drilling, feeling gravel and powder between his fingers, no way to proceed. He slept fitfully, woke screaming, dreamed about earthquakes. A few months later, when I became pregnant again, Dan found a psychiatrist and started taking Celexa, to try to right his moods. Up until that point he'd continued to feel sure that if he did not complete our seismic retrofit one day that the Big One would hit the next and we'd lose everything. At the same time he'd felt positive that the tie-down bolts were useless at best, and that all he was doing down there in the basement was securing our nest egg to a pile of sand.

In the intervening years, Dan and I had tried hard to be gentle with each other, pursuing what might be called a de facto marital acceptance strategy. Dan would chuckle—or at least try to chuckle—about my dysfunction regarding compliments (not only at my inability to give them but my lack of grace in receiving them. I tended to regard compliments as ploys for me to praise him back). In return he'd suggest I say something along the lines of, "Oh you lovable, obsessive man, you!" when he lectured me, again, about periodized weight training and why I should start working on my dead lift, bench press, and squat. This approach was similar to integrative behavioral couple therapy, in which couples work on "change-oriented strategies," trying to fix each partner's maladaptive habits, and when those aren't enough, they switch to "acceptance work," attempting to learn to love the relationship as is.

But Holly, weighing in from her chaise longue in her office, took the straight-up fix-it, or at least diagnose-it, approach. "No, no, no," she said, near the end of that first session, concerning Dan's desire for me to view his rants as sweet. "She doesn't want to be a sounding board. She wants to feel that you see her as a person, that you're checking in with her."

This was true: I loathed feeling disregarded and anonymous. But I also believed the marriage research that put value on the positive. I liked the infiltrations of positive psychology into couples' therapy, the studies that found forgiveness to be key to marital satisfaction, the finding that supportiveness buoys a marriage more than negativity drags it down. Holly's view painted Dan not as a charming obsessive but an anxious neurotic. Still, we decided to continue seeing her. She was incisive, if acerbic. She made us think. Our second session, the following week, ended with this cutting synopsis. "On the one hand," Holly said, "you find Dan unavailable because he's not relating to you. You think he just wants something from you. But on the other hand he feels he can't reach you, either. He wants you to accept his affection and praise, but those attentions make you feel smothered, and that makes him feel alone."

Two fifty-minute sessions of therapy, and Holly had reduced our pretty-good marriage to an unappealing, maybe even unsalvageable conundrum. Would her vote of little confidence really help? After leaving her office I stopped in the bathroom to change into my running clothes. Dan, far more practiced at therapy than I was, waited outside in the hallway then walked me down the stairs. "Do you think they spray shrink powder in this place?" he asked. "You know, to make it extra depressing?"

His arm around my shoulders felt heavy and strong. His tone was protective, chivalrous. As we walked down Sacramento Street, he took Holly's darkness and transferred it right back at her. "And what's wrong with that lady, anyway? She reminds me of Stephen Hawking."

6

Marriage Education

D an and I didn't expect much when we signed up for a sixteen-
hour, two-Saturday marriage education class called Mastering the
Mysteries of Love. Actually, that's not true: We expected to hate it. Two
days trapped in a government-sponsored curriculum on how to conduct
an intimate relationship? That sounded awful, like a cross between
drivers ed and being chastised by Hannah for doing her laundry wrong.

But the class also sounded perfect for me, at least in principle. The
godfather of marriage education, a psychologist named Bernard Guerney, believed just what I wanted to believe: that you can learn to be
better at marriage, that marriage is a teachable skill. "Unless the client
is suffering a biochemical deficiency or imbalance, he is no more sick
than someone who wants to play tennis but does not know how, and
the professional is no more providing 'therapy' and 'curing' his or her
clients than the coach is 'curing' his 'client,' " Guerney wrote in his 1977
book, *Relationship Enhancement.* So one drizzly morning, several weeks
after we'd started seeing Holly, Dan and I dropped the girls off with my
mother and crossed the Golden Gate Bridge.

Since 2006, the U.S. Department of Health and Human Services had been promoting marriage classes, part of an effort Katherine Boo brilliantly described in a *New Yorker* article as the "marriage cure." The idea was straightforward: married Americans tended to be richer, happier, healthier, and more stable—and raise richer, happier, healthier, and more stable children; therefore, matrimony must be an efficient palliative for social and financial woes. (Unfortunately, this reasoning was flawed. Richer, happier, healthier, and more stable people are the ones who tend to get married, and if you control who marries, almost all the benefits of marriage, even to children born in wedlock, disappear.) The second Bush administration earmarked $100 million a year for five years for marriage education. The California Healthy Marriage Initiative won the largest grant.

"See? Look at them," I said to Dan as we parked near the base of Mount Tam in the salt-and-eucalyptus–scented air. We had both felt ashamed to be coming to this class. Wasn't marriage education for poor people, or people who didn't understand relationships, or miserable couples who wanted to be able to tell themselves they'd tried everything yet not learned anything specific? Now a great-looking couple about our age was walking just ahead of us down the narrow canopied road bumping each other's arms and hips. "They look happy. And normal. And self-respecting."

Then, as the fog collected into rain, that couple turned into the wrong driveway. Bounding down from the address we'd been given came a young man who appeared to have stepped out of Terrence Malik's *Days of Heaven*—handsome, strong, and sad. He wore a too-small denim shirt and carried a sleep-deprived, nearly feral look in his eyes. He waved at us, cringing with self-loathing. "Just follow the balloons!" he said.

To start the day our instructor, Keith—a late middle-aged corporate communication consultant with a very dignified British accent—offered us glasses of cucumber water, presumably prepared by his wife, Deborah, who ran a day spa downstairs. Keith and Deborah had recently

53

completed Mastering the Mysteries of Love and a sixteen-hour teacher training course. Deborah's beauty clients often asked her for relationship advice. She wanted to offer them "something real."

Turns out marriage education appeals to the practical-minded. After introductions, Keith asked the *Days of Heaven* man and his equally sad, strong, and gutted-looking wife to stand back-to-back and take turns describing the world as they saw it.

The *Days of Heaven* man gazed toward the front of Keith's nice house, out the large windows facing the Marin Headlands, now being glazed with rain. The *Days of Heaven* man said, "I see spirals, trees, a kitty pillow on a bench. . . ."

"And is that what you see?" Keith asked the wife.

"No," she said, torso buried in her Dickie's sweatshirt, hands fiddling with her diamond ring. "That's not what the world looks like to me at all. In my world there's an Asian cupboard, a deck with a hot tub, and two hummingbirds playing."

"Oh, hummingbirds!" Deborah, the aesthetician, clapped. "That's a good omen!"

The *Days of Heaven* husband deadpanned, without turning around, "Those birds aren't playing. One's attacking the other."

Keith then laid out our goal for the day: to learn how to have "skilled conversations"—as opposed to the rhetorical jousting matches standard in many relationships and around our house. A skilled conversation is an exercise in forced empathy. One person starts by describing his or her feelings—and as Keith reminded, "If you can substitute '*I think*' for '*I feel*,' it's not a feeling. 'I feel like you're an asshole' is not a feeling." The other person validates those feelings, perhaps even repeating them verbatim.

I had insecurities galore—klutziness, dancing, ineptitude with a hair dryer, inability to believe in, and thus pull off, sexy lingerie. But talking? I could talk. Dan could, too. A whole sector of the marriage-improvement world is devoted to communication skills, to devising verbal gimmicks to remind husbands and wives to use with each other the same good social graces they employ with everybody else. Listen. Precede criticism with praise. Avoid exaggeration. Stick to the facts. To reinstall these habits in marriage, one class uses a "talking mat," sort of like the mat in Twister; another uses a schema called the "Daily Temperature Reading," a conversational road map that starts with "appreciation," moves to "puzzles" (as in, "I'm puzzled. I thought you were going to come home at 7:00 p.m. and here it is 8:15 p.m."), then ends pleasantly with "wishes, hopes, and dreams." I didn't feel enthusiastic about talking in a template. Still, I decided the best thing to do was just stick it out when Keith assigned us our first drill: to take turns telling our spouses childhood stories, then retell those stories *as if we were our spouses,* emphasizing in our retellings how the events made us feel.

Keith dismissed us from the dining room table to find a private corner in his home. Walking through his kitchen, Dan clucked with approval at the hanging conical strainers. Then we settled in the den on a love seat, near a picture window through which we could watch the soft rain fall. I felt so happy to be alone with Dan. I always felt close to him in situations like this. We could be in an airport, or at an awkward dinner party, anything borderline unpleasant or dull. I'd catch Dan's infinity-pool eyes, now framed by crow's-feet I'd watched grow myself, and think, *Thank god.*

Dan now took my hands and said, "You ready?" He looked earnest and composed.

"Ready," I said.

Dan then told me a small and awkward story, one that I'd never heard, because it's not the kind of story I respond to well. When Dan was eight or nine years old, the city of Berkeley tore up the playground across the street from his house to install new structures. For a time the lot was filled with dirt clods, which the neighborhood boys used for "dirt clod wars." Dan played along most days after school. But one afternoon he decided to quit early, and another boy followed him back across the street, to the Duanes' house, still throwing dirt. "So I picked up this clod to throw back at him, or at least I thought it was a clod. But I had this flicker in my mind that the dirt felt too heavy, that it had to contain a rock." Dan threw it anyway. He hit the boy's eye. "It was awful," Dan said, still holding my hands. "I really hurt that kid. I had this horrible feeling of shame."

Then, my turn: "Okay," I started out. "When you were a boy . . ."

"Don't say *you,*" Keith interrupted. I'd been too absorbed in Dan's story to notice that Keith had entered the room. "*Be* Dan. Tell the story *as* Dan," Keith said. "Don't offer him sympathy. Just connect."

I started again. *Be Dan?* For a story about pelting a boy with a rock? I'd made a point of keeping my distance from the aggressive side of Dan. I felt uncomfortable with the part of him that screamed at people who left barking dogs tied to parking meters, the part that sought out conflict. But Dan had told this story, and here we were at marriage class—I needed to shed my judgment and smugness (signs I was afraid of my own aggressiveness?) and give the exercise a try. "So, I, as Dan, was over in Totland one day when I was eight or nine, and we were all having this big dirt clod war." And so on—the kid, the rock, the throw, the eye. I felt transported speaking from my new vantage point, closer to Dan. I did not expect to feel such change. I finished by saying, "I felt so guilty and humiliated."

"Oh my god," Dan said. "Do that again."

"Do what?" I asked.

"Do *that,*" he said, his eyes wide. "Do that whole thing that you just did." He'd experienced something extremely personal, too. "You never talk to me like that. I think you must really love me."

We expect intimacy to bloom over time. But we also know it can be forced—the freshman orientation camping trip, the corporate team-building trust fall. This trick, too—telling each other's stories—felt like closeness rigged, then tripped on command. I didn't like feeling so easily played, but the exercise had worked.

The skilled conversation also made me realize what a wretched empath I often am. Sure, I listen when Dan speaks. I can often repeat his words back verbatim. Yet most of the time when I do this— *this is the apartment building you lived in that summer your group of high school friends really did have four weddings and a funeral*—I'm just rewinding the tape, not inhabiting Dan's experience, certainly not digging underneath his words to find his core emotional truth. But as I retold Dan's dirt clod tale, I felt my identification shift. My job was not to comment, nor move the conversation forward. My job was only to empathize. I felt like I'd climbed out of the bunker in which I usually live and run over to Dan's bunker, to be with him there.

This felt new. One of the most confounding parts of marriage for me was determining how much emotional distance to put between myself and Dan, particularly when one or both of us was hurting. This problem mushroomed the summer after we aborted the baby, when Dan plunged into darkness, falling at a rate for which I was unprepared. That July—2004—I'd been telling myself we were getting back on our feet. Dan wanted to believe this, too. Emerging from the basement, he even had the presence of mind to suggest we go backpacking in the Sierra Nevada. My parents could come watch Hannah, and Dan and I could reconnect.

The Sierra, for us, was a geographic touchstone, one of those places we returned to again and again, what T. S. Eliot called a "still point of the turning world." We'd spent a week amid the meadows and ice-cold lakes each summer we'd been together. In the past the Sierra had provided me with joy, solace, a much-needed wake-up call, hope, lucidity, and even a sweet form of regret. But the first day of our trip, that summer after our loss, Dan and I fought horribly.

Shouldering my backpack out of dusty Devil's Postpile, I felt different from previous years—worse. Not only physically older, though I felt that, too. I felt scared of facing myself. Scared of facing Dan. Less than a mile from the trailhead I wanted to leave.

"I'm not sure Hannah's ready for us to be gone this long," I said, setting down my backpack to rest.

"This isn't about Hannah. Hannah will be fine."

"But she's so young. And we've been so screwed up."

"Sweetheart, listen to me," Dan said, turning my sweaty shoulders to face him. "Hannah's fine. *You're* not fine. *We're* not fine. We need this."

We walked in silence over the angular bricks of basalt. I resumed pleading my case at mile two.

"But we've never both been gone for this long."

"Hannah's fine," Dan said again, wringing out the last of his patience. "She won't even notice."

At mile three I started once more. Dan finally snapped.

"Will you please cut the bullshit?" he said, spreading his arms out toward the trees, as if he could block the exit. "This is *not* about Hannah. This is about us. We're strung out pretty fucking far here. You've been gone, totally gone for two years now. You were gone when you were pregnant, and I understood that. And you were gone when Hannah was born, and I understood that, too. And now you've disappeared down some dark fucking rabbit hole. I need you, baby. *I* need *you*. Don't do this. Don't run away."

I closed my eyes. I knew he was right. I needed to find a way to cling to Dan despite the fact that when I looked at him now I saw all my pain. I couldn't face talking, so I just nodded and walked through the heat—uncomfortably, up the switchbacks, Dan monitoring me close behind. On day two, reaching our campsite, I felt my shoulders relax for the first time in months, and the next evening, renewed by a freezing swim, I even felt like myself from previous years—happily exhausted, humbled by the beauty, and eager for our standard mountain cocktail: a nip of whiskey from a plastic flask and a few salted nuts. We didn't talk about the son we didn't have. I read *The Devil Wears Prada* to Dan aloud. On our last night out, a dozen horses galloped up Lyell Canyon to pasture, and the unexpected vitality, the clomping speed, made us tuck into the lodgepole pines, trying to conceive a child again. Our water pump broke on our last morning, but on the walk out a hiker offered us half a dripping cantaloupe. We'd made it through a passage, turned a corner. Or so I thought.

But within a week back home, that summer of 2004, Dan was waking at 4:30 a.m. Plus he'd started "self-medicating," as he called it: two-hour gym sessions that included lifting weights while kneeling on a Swiss ball, and squatting and leaping again and again in a move he called "jumpies," also with weights in hand. He'd even reverted to his careful meting out of caffeine and alcohol—part of a Berkeley faith in better living through chemistry. He looked so strong, and he hurt so much inside.

In late August we flew to Boston, to meet my extended family at a lodge in Maine. I knew Dan was fragile emotionally, and that the prospect of five days away from his scripted routes, trapped inland on a lake with my investment banker brother, made him tense. Still, once through airport security, Dan fetched us coffee and muffins, his normal travel routine. He asked Hannah her favorite question, "Kisses or tickles?" We boarded the plane.

By the time we'd landed at Logan Airport, Dan was starting to come unglued. He'd muttered anxiously for an hour about the turbulence, and the first thing he said as we walked out of the terminal to my father's car was "The air smells different" in a way I could tell he didn't like. As always he did an amazing job of projecting surfer mellow, so much so that my parents noticed nothing, and he even managed to charm Hannah to sleep in the car, narrating for her the walks they always took together up Bernal Hill, waving at the boats on San Francisco Bay and Dan's childhood home across it.

Still, as we drove the two hours north to Sebago Lake I could feel Dan was an explosion in search of a fuse. He'd never grieved outwardly. He'd just supported me until I could fake resuming normal life, then we'd moved on. But I knew he thought about that baby boy all the time, and that the pain remained sharp. My brother would be meeting us at Migis Lodge—with his two sons. Everything en route felt like an affront: the Red Sox game on the radio, the Friendly's restaurant restroom. Each slowdown in traffic threatened to break Dan's mood. I wanted a vacation, I needed a vacation. I did not need an unstable, heartbroken, angry husband, and following what Dan described as my "slamma-jamma method of housecleaning"—i.e., making pretty surfaces by shoving junk into drawers—I tried to pretend that I did not have one now. Minutes after we reached Migis, I grabbed half-awake Hannah and marched down the foot trail to the rocky beach, desperate to secure a canoe trip to my favorite dock before the blast hit.

Our first night there Dan didn't sleep. The place is lovely and old school, with cabins in the woods, picnic lunches on a granite point, maple sugar lemonade, water-skiing at ten and two. I'd been visiting the lodge with my parents since my teens. In the past Dan had enjoyed Migis, too. Yes, he'd felt simmering tensions with my brother. Most summers David would make an offhand remark about Dan wearing a wool sport coat in July, or he'd gloat over winning a sailing race—jabs that cut worse than they might have given the economic disparity. But money was only part of the problem. My brother and I had been very close through our early twenties, but even by the time we shared that triple-decker in Cambridge, our lives had started diverging, our trajectories splaying outward, and in marriage we'd declared our separation final. In our spouses we'd chosen privately—not just professionally—very different paths. Dan was not much like my brother. My brother's wife, while lovely, was not much like me. We never discussed this—the choices we made in marriage—but I think we both felt a little bruised that the other had not picked a person more like ourselves.

That first day in Migis, Dan and David gave each other a wide berth. My brother and his wife, Cindy, shared a cabin with their boys. My sister had a room in the lodge with her fiancé. All of us interacted carefully, trying to figure out how to be a family, to embrace our new in-laws, these spouses we did not choose. But early on our first morning, Dan arose, sleepless, and tied on his running shoes for a five-mile jog. Then he set out on a predawn row. When he finished, his mind still unquiet, he swam out to a small island in the lake and back.

I thought I knew what Dan was feeling: lost in the foreign universe in another family. I sometimes felt this with the Duanes. But when Dan swam back, the sun midway up the sky, he was more than just disoriented by his in-laws. He was ready to snap. Late morning, still too tense to sit for breakfast, Dan marched off to spend the day doing god knows what. I headed the other direction, with Hannah, to ride the boat at the ski dock.

Should I have followed Dan instead? Joined him in his misery? I was not very stable myself. I didn't want to bunker down with Dan in his pain. Shouldn't I complete my own rescue before attempting his? Some friends of mine had divorced after the death of their daughter. Their grief had transformed them into those wretched climbing partners in *Touching the Void*, one of whom had broken his leg when the other accidentally lowered him, on belay, off a cliff. Pulling the man with the broken leg back up to safety was not an option. The best chance for either to survive was for the higher, healthier man to cut the rope. (Amazingly, both lived. The man with the broken leg fell a hundred feet into a crevasse. He then crawled for three days without food or water to reach base camp.)

That evening, in our cabin at Migis, I put on a black skirt and sandals, then walked over the needles to the lodge for a much-needed drink. Dan said he wanted to come—a good sign. On the veranda, we drained our gin and tonics. My brother David and his wife showed up. Everyone discussed Michael Moore's *Fahrenheit 9/11*, and at some point in the conversation—nobody can remember the trigger—David called one of Dan's comments "moronic." That was how my brother talked, in those years: conversation as a contact sport. But this was just the slight for which Dan had been waiting. He kept his anger contained through appetizers in the dining room with my parents. Then, after I excused myself to check on Hannah and the babysitter, Dan asked David to step outside. There, through some French doors, in full view of my whole family (or so all parties reported), Dan grabbed David's shirt collar and told him never to call him a moron in front of his wife again.

"I didn't call you a moron," David said, rattled.

"Yes, you did."

Dan listed the insults David had dealt him over the years. Then, still holding my brother's collar, he told him it was over: no more talking to him that way.

"Are you going to punch me?" David asked.

"Do you want me to?" Dan's question was cruel. He released David's collar. Dan took off at a trot.

An hour later, when I found him up the long drive, Dan was still shaking. All of our personalities creak from time to time, but my husband's whole self had fallen off its hinges. He sat on a boulder, clutching his hair, pupils oddly tiny despite the dark. He needed my support and affection—that was very clear. And I remember thinking, despite my fury, "This is the part, this is really being married," and hoping I could be true both to myself and to Dan at the same time. Dan was suffering. I was angry. We were four years into marriage, according to the Relationship Institute at UCLA the nadir for many couples, especially for wives. I had no reserves, or thought I had none.

A small fraction of the problem was also cultural. When Dan was in elementary school, his Irish father had advised him that if you think a fight might turn physical, take the first swing. This was not the received wisdom in my family. Its intrusion did not go over well now. Yet I'd bound myself to this person, agreed to run through life joined, as in a three-legged race. Should I try to shoulder Dan's weight for the stretch that lay ahead? Should I fall to the ground with him? Should I cut and run? We sat on the granite under the stars, Dan's cheek wet with tears on my knees. I felt small and in too deep, far over my head. I always knew Dan's body might crumble someday. I had not considered the impermanence of his graceful mind.

Back on the love seat in Mill Valley in marriage class, five years later, I started telling a childhood story to Dan. "One day, in the spring of sixth grade, I wore red cotton shorts to school."

I'd had a hard time thinking of an anecdote, to be honest. I talked very little about growing up in Wellesley.

"After lunch our teachers, Miss Dickie and Mrs. Lane, asked all of the students to pull chairs to the front of the room. They wanted to show a film strip, and there, in the dark, surrounded by the other kids, I noticed my thighs spreading across my seat." This was the same year that I'd sprouted breasts, an advancement I'd met with horror, so much so that I refused to wear a bra. My mother, who possessed a real bosom, responded with a two-layer rule: two shirts, shirt plus sweatshirt, bra plus shirt, any two. I didn't mind the rule, but I was scared of my growing body, scared of growing up.

When I finished speaking Dan kept his eyes locked onto mine. This was not the kind of story he typically related to, either. As a child, he couldn't wait to be a man, to be just like his father. Still, he took his job of retelling my story seriously.

"One spring when I was in the sixth grade, I wore red shorts to school. . . ."

Sweet Jesus! For years I'd been the object of Dan's affection. Now

I was the subject. I know this sounds cerebral and academic, but with Dan speaking as me, as the subject, I felt from him such intense loyalty, felt he was truly by my side. I did not feel watched or appreciated (both nice, but distant). I felt *joined.* The space between us folded flat, like the sides of a box. I cried with relief.

Later that day, with the gongs of the supposedly soothing spa music crashing in the background, Keith instructed us to have a skilled conversation about a "small disagreement." Suffice it to say, this was not the form we'd previously defaulted to when discussing how much weekend time to spend at my parents' Napa condo, a place Dan often described as "that totally sterile golf community in which your mother feeds our kids Popsicles for breakfast and I'm forbidden to cook." I know, I know: We should all be blessed with such problems. And we knew we were. Still, our past several dozen run-ins on the topic had not gone well, in part because we didn't ally with each other. Why would I ally with Dan? My mother did not *always* feed our kids Popsicles for breakfast; she sometimes let him cook. Dan's hyperbole piqued my defenses and scuttled my goodwill. So I dismissed his concerns, along with his right to influence how his children spent their weekends, by saying, "Fine, don't go."

I told myself my attitude was justified, even altruistic. I was taking Hannah and Audrey to Napa, right? Dan could boil goats' feet or scream at motorists or do whatever the hell else he wanted with his free time. But now, following the Mastering the Mysteries of Love template, Dan was saying—and I was repeating—that these weekends at my parents' condo made him feel alienated and left out of decision-making in our family. (I had not even realized this was a decision-making issue to him.) And I was saying, and he was repeating, that spending time with my parents meant the world to me. Our children loved being with them, and my parents were still healthy. I knew this couldn't last.

We didn't sound funny or clever. Neither of us "won" the conversation or even scored any points. Yet as we spoke in that earnest, nearly cloying style, I felt a trapdoor crack open in the back corner of our marriage—real progress at last. The feeling remained throughout the afternoon. We discussed back rubs, parallel parking, the crushing banality of married life. Dan would confess something small—say, that he felt unappreciated when I collected the breakfast dishes and left them piled in the sink, as this made it difficult for him to cook. Instinct demanded I defend myself, but instead I choked back my reasons and parroted back Dan's feelings: "You feel unconsidered and disregarded when . . ." We felt that oh-my-god-you-*do*-really-understand-me sensation of falling in love.

At 5:00 p.m., we left to return to the city, euphoric and a bit stunned. How had a cheap rhetorical trick to manufacture unconditional allegiance made us feel so connected? More to the point, how could we have been shutting each other out emotionally—*not* identifying, *not* fully allying, for years—and not even known it? Never in our marriage had I questioned our joking banter or suspected that we used it to bury uncomfortable feelings. But clearly we had. And now that we'd set it aside, back at home that first irony-free evening, my whole suburban adolescence came pouring out. The girls bathed, their stories read, Dan and I lounged on our bed and I began telling childhood stories, pulling them out in an uninterrupted stream like a magician who tugs a corner of cloth from his cheek and finds a five-yard-long scarf.

My parents had given me what they'd known how to give: eight weeks of summer overnight camp, a good education, unconditional love and trust. But as was now obvious, for years I hadn't talked about my childhood much because I'd felt uneasy and insecure. I'd grown up a geek in a family of even bigger geeks. Without an ironclad guarantee of empathy—an assurance that no jokes about the debate club or my regrets at not having joined it would be made at my expense—I felt my stories could not compete with Dan's sun-drenched epics about skateboarding and throwing Frisbees in Berkeley's Tilden Park.

But now I felt exhilarated to be airing my antiheroics. The upstairs of our house was public space, where we ate roast chickens and I chatted with Dan's mother on Mondays after she'd picked up Hannah and Audrey from school. But downstairs was private, easier to uncork. Below, I was just a wife—not a mother, not a friend, not a daughter or daughter-in-law. I was often in a nightgown, supine, as I was now. Staring at the ceiling I lit into my own stream-of-consciousness analysis, telling Dan that in my childhood memories (undoubtedly skewed) my father long maintained the fantasy that I was popular because I had a so-called friend named Cindy who kept a horse, alongside her mother's horse, at a nearby riding stable. But really, as I saw it, I was just barely hanging on, permitted to talk to the non-dorks in the halls of Wellesley Middle School but not to join them afterward at Friendly's for grilled cheese and Cokes.

The apex of my embarrassment was my bat mitzvah. I'd always felt pressured to have one, though neither of my parents said flat out, *Please, do this for me.* Now I was supposed to invite my supposed friends to synagogue, with my family? And then stand up in a Laura Ashley dress with a frilly stand-up collar, a look not helped by my bowl haircut, which I somehow managed to feather through the near-criminal use of a hair dryer? Still, the worst part, as I explained to Dan, was not the ceremony or the reception following but the DJ dance party the next evening in my parents' basement. What delusional fit of pubescent hubris had given me the impression I could pull this off? I couldn't dance. Nobody in my family could dance. The only good dancing I'd ever seen was on *Solid Gold,* and unlike Dan in Berkeley, I lacked the forethought to practice along. As I descended the two sets of stairs, from my bedroom with the periwinkle curtains to the orange-plaid-carpeted cellar, I realized I'd made a horrendous mistake. I was wearing teal pedal pushers and a teal asymmetrical ruffled shirt. My goal was to slow dance with Gary Zimble, my best friend's older brother, to the Journey anthem "Open Arms."

Needless to say, this didn't happen.

"Honey!" Dan shouted when I finished. "Why haven't you been telling me all this? It's great stuff."

The relief of telling the stories spilled into sex.

For that day at least, we'd managed to side with each other emotionally, no matter what, and that led us to be more trusting physically and more exposed.

7

Intimacy

"Hey. . . . Yeah. . . . Is this . . . Liz?"

Don Flecky, our marriage education coach, had called. Don was a building contractor outside Los Angeles. He also worked, part-time, for the California Healthy Marriage Initiative. The group often cited research from conservative think tanks bemoaning how expensive divorce was for society. One report put the expense to American taxpayers of family fragmentation at $112 billion a year. The promise of the marriage cure was to reduce such costs (though nobody proved it did). So once a week for six weeks, Don, our coach, called me and Dan at home. The idea was to make our marriage education move effectively, to coax us into having skilled conversations in our daily lives.

This was good. I needed the encouragement, as by the time Don rang, just five days after our first session of Mastering the Mysteries of Love, I had started growing hypoxic in Dan's emotional bunker, dizzy from living, in that saccharine phrase of marriage improvement, as "we instead of me." That week had felt so intimate and intense—this was the goal, right?—all my energy and Dan's rushing toward each other. But some mornings following intimate nights I'd find myself pulling on my jeans and T-shirt more slowly than usual, pausing before I joined our family in the sunny kitchen upstairs. Now adding to my feeling of suffocation: Don talked slowly. Incredibly slowly. The minute I heard his voice my chest began to constrict.

"Hey . Yeah. . . . Hi. . . . And Is . . . Dan . . . there . . . too?"

"Hey, Don," Dan said.

The two of us sat side by side on the carpeted floor of my office, each holding a cordless phone with a headset attached. I inhaled deeply, then sighed. Don's studied calm brought out my hypertension. Within two sentences I felt like a driver who'd had the misfortune of tailgating my own mellow-on-the-outside, wound-up-on-the-inside husband. His response to being followed was not to speed up or switch lanes but to slow down and tap the brake.

Please don't get me wrong: I liked Don, our marriage coach. I later met him in a café in Westwood, before a marriage class he'd invited me to help facilitate, and I found him charming, easy to talk to, and warm. But on the phone his words stretched through time and space like an invading country. "Some . . . people . . . find . . . the . . . skills . . . are . . . awkward . . . at . . . first . . . as . . . they're . . . learning . . . them. . . . Did . . . you . . . find . . . that?"

I enjoyed this western patois in Cormac McCarthy novels. I especially loved Ed Tom Bell, the character played by Tommy Lee Jones in the film version of *No Country for Old Men*, a sheriff who responds to simple yes-or-no questions with obtuse non-answers like, "Probably I do." But in real life, especially right now, Don's dawdling drawl frayed my nerves. I'd made peace with living in California. (Dan never wavered on his unwillingness to move.) My parents had even relocated to San Francisco, renting an apartment in the Marina district in the summer of 2005, shortly after Audrey's birth. But just like some people slip into their childhood southern or Brooklyn accents when slightly drunk, anxiety made me cling to my native cadence. I answered Don's question in double time, sounding like I'd toked on a helium balloon.

"A little bit. I liked this analogy that Keith, our marriage-class teacher, used, how learning these skills is like learning to drive a car. They're really awkward and preoccupying at first, and you have to focus on the mechanics and you feel like a clumsy goon. But the goal is to stop thinking. You know, have the skills be second nature and just do them in the background."

Don responded with a minute-long, "Y e a h. . . ."

I now realize Don irritated me because I was scared of giving over more of myself, especially to a man who embodied the West. That week, when I'd ascend tardily to the kitchen, Dan would caress the small of my back. I'd squirm away. My main objective, while making coffee and braiding the girls' hair, was to return to being me and me alone. Dan had such an enormous personality. I loved this about him, but it made me panic. I didn't want to solve the riddle of marriage—the Sphinx-like conundrum of how to be two people and yet one—with the dreamy but suffocating $1 + 1 = 1$. I hadn't really figured out who I was and what life I wanted to live until I was in my early twenties, and I didn't want to spend the remainder of that life thinking and feeling as Dan. I wanted $1 + 1 = 2$, the antiromantic math.

I was also jealous of my personal boundaries due to earlier missteps. I'd worried I'd given over too much to Dan since that day along the Charles River when I'd lost the negotiation about where to live. Had I taken too literally Thomas Merton's philosophy that "love demands a complete inner transformation. . . . We [must] become, in a sense, the person we love"? Before and during our engagement I'd driven with Dan to the beach nearly every surfable day.

For the first few weeks I ran along the bike path while Dan rode waves. Then we'd huddle together on the dune at the end of Taraval Street, Dan teaching me how to read the ocean, how to parse the bands of blue-black energy as they pulsed through the water, stood up, curled, and crashed. When a good wave broke, Dan shook his head and said, "Shoooooo doggy." *Shooooo doggy?* Who spoke like this? Still, when Dan asked me if I wanted to learn to surf, I said yes.

Lesson one was that surfing involves long hours of checking the surf. Driving south to Santa Cruz, toward the gentler waves, Dan and I stopped at four breaks—Four Mile, Three Mile, Scott's, Ledges—all before renting me a wet suit from a tourist shack in town. Once in the water, Dan slid me his nine-six—nine and a half feet of fiberglassed Styrofoam, painted with red hibiscus flowers—and told me, patiently, that he was going to push me, atop the board, into the lines of rushing white water. The white water would then carry me shoreward, giving me a taste of the water's energy and speed.

I was hooked from the start, though I didn't like the only beginner break we could reach most days after work, a beach called Linda Mar, just twenty minutes south of the city. At Linda Mar derelicts and hormonal teenagers lined the cement windbreak. Conversations took place in the lowest common denominator and tended to go like this:

"Kinda gnarly, huh?"

"Yeah, but it's bitchin'."

"That guy's killing it."

"Fully."

One day Dan and I met a man who claimed to be a poet. He'd just heard about an exciting new book: "Roget's *Thesaurus*. It has lots of words."

I was tongue-tied. Dan stepped in.

"Yeah," he said, nodding to the poet. "You should get it. It's bitchin'."

Turns out Don, our telephone marriage coach, had grown up on surfing, too. He spoke in the flat lugubrious rhythms of Sean Penn's Spicoli in *Fast Times at Ridgemont High*. But the truth is he was helpful in his protracted way. As Dan shifted from sitting to lying supine on the office floor, Don asked us to pick up a discussion topic, something to "enhance" our marriage. Dan, ever obsessive, suggested our how-many-summer-weekends-to-spend-at-my-parents-condo-in-Napa problem—no closure there yet.

"Dan," Don said, gently shooting down the idea, "that . . . sounds . . . like . . . a . . . conflict . . . topic . . . to . . . me."

So we moved on to Dan's gripe that we didn't hire babysitters to go on dates more often.

Babysitters! What a farce. We both knew why we didn't hire baby-sitters more: We spent five days a week home alone together during the day, and when we did hire sitters the imperative to have fun, right then, because the meter was running—*tick tick tick*—often ruined the night. We agreed on this. We even performed our stressed-out date-night rap at dinner parties, to knowing laughs. The date night was nothing like a real date—so little potential to be unnerved or surprised, so little chance of real romance. Real romance requires an element of the unknown (difficult to pull off with babysitter scheduling), personal revelation, and authentic risk. Lately, on our best dates, something had gone wrong—the car broke down so we walked through the Mission, or the restaurant lost our reservation so we drove up to Twin Peaks with takeout and watched the moon over the city instead. But now, with marriage-coach Don on the line, my husband had cast himself as the father of young kids who never sees his wife and thus needs to pay someone to watch the kids so he can speak to his beloved on Saturday night. More annoying, given the pretense, Dan was performing this role in a pronoun form I called "the marital we."

The marital we was not the "royal we," an ego-inflated I. This was a *we* that really meant *you,* as in (Dan speaking to me), "Why don't we," that is, *you*—"hire babysitters more?" Over the years we'd also cultivated a *we* that really meant *I,* as in (Dan speaking) "*We* haven't decided what to have for dinner yet." But I spared Don the fine points of our semantics. Instead I engaged with Dan in a skilled but bogus fight, which began with him offering to hire a sitter for Saturday night and my parrying with the news that Saturday was his father's birthday and we were expected for dinner at the Duanes', which he already knew. I then suggested that "we" could see if Audrey's old nanny could come over that night, right after work. But Dan demurred. Of course he did. He didn't actually want to hire a sitter. He wanted to see our kids. This was the real reason we (I) didn't hire more nighttime help. We—the real we, the two of us—spent kid-free workdays together, the dividend of our otherwise questionable careers. I loved our days. We talked, really talked—about our work, about our lives. We even took a "micro-date" most days after lunch, walking down to the bakery for tea or a treat. We (the real we) believed that evenings, especially weekday evenings, were the girls' time. One of my roles in our marriage was to protect this time for them. But when I abandoned the position, Dan stepped in.

Don's job was not to counsel, just to help us maintain a structured conversation. Finally we all hung up and could resume speaking like ourselves. "Oh my god, honey," I said to Dan, apologizing, "I'm so sorry I dragged you into this whole marriage project. That guy's voice . . . Didn't he just drive you crazy?"

Dan had no idea what I was talking about. The project, shockingly, wasn't bothering him. He enjoyed both therapy and learning new techniques. He also dropped the idea of hiring a sitter.

"Really?" he said. "I like that guy."

That spring, as the wind gusted, scrubbing the coast, I kept experiencing the psychological equivalent of Newton's Third Law of Motion. I felt an innate equal-and-opposite reaction to our newfound closeness, to living "as we instead of me." I really did like the idea of empathy—even compulsory empathy—to a point. But as was becoming clear, for me the marriage mathematics weren't as simple as the more intimacy, the better. If Dan and I were going to have more intimacy, I was going to need more autonomy, too.

Like many women I knew, I'd read a few years back, in fascinated horror, a *New York Times* article about a Buddhist couple in the Arizona desert who'd taken vows never to part by more than fifteen feet. They inhaled and exhaled in unison while doing yoga, walked each other to writing desks when inspiration struck in the middle of the night. "It's very intimate," the male partner explained. And that vision of intimacy, as a chain-link leash, filled me with existential dread. Yes, I loved the emotional security of knowing if I said, "I'm upset," Dan would repeat back, "You're upset." But while I found this command empathy instructive, even comforting and useful to a point, it also felt unsustainable and cloying.

Much of the conversation about what distinguishes a so-so or good marriage from a great marriage involves the distinction between loving one's spouse and being "in love"—a state academics call "limerence." In her 2003 screed *Against Love,* Laura Kipnis describes that change as a domestication, from lion on the Serengeti to "house-trained kitten." She views this as inevitable and wretched, a path leading to "the nagging voice at the end of your well-being. . . . The one that says, *'Isn't there supposed to be something more?'*" When Al and Tipper Gore split in the summer of 2010, PR teams on both sides spun variations on a single theme: "It doesn't even mean they don't love each other anymore. They're just not in love." But, honestly, how could they have been, or at least how could they have remained continuously "in love," through forty years, the near-death of their son, and two presidential bids? As anthropologist Helen Fisher writes in her acclaimed book *Why We Love,* being "in love" is not a feeling, it's "a psychological need." Brain scans of lovers read as pathological, addled by cravings as strong as drug addiction, hunger, and thirst. In fact, lovers are functionally addicts, hooked on dopamine and norepinephrine—which may not be all that different from being hooked on methamphetamines, as meth works by blocking reuptake of the former two compounds, causing people to feel ecstatic and not eat. Unfortunately, the cocktail of dopamine and norepinephrine seems to work on the human brain for only twelve to eighteen months. Then, for nearly everyone, the in-love experience fades.

But maybe it's not so bad, really. And what if Al Gore or his fellow leaders really remained in love? Just witness the professional swan dive of the South Carolina "Love Guv" Mark Sanford, who disappeared for six days, supposedly to "hike the Appalachian Trail," while really he was in Argentina, admiring his lover's tan lines, BlackBerry disengaged. When he returned to face his constituents, he stood at the Charleston podium, blissed out past decorum. "I'll die knowing I met my soul mate," he told the assembled throng. A lovely feeling for Sanford in the moment, but who the hell would vote for him?

While Dan and I were falling in love, our world and our fan base shrunk, too, partly because we extracted from each other a sort of ritual sacrifice in the form of each other's friends. This sounds horrible, and it was, but it seemed to be happening with a lot of engaged or soon-to-be-engaged couples we knew at the time: a game of premarital Texas Hold 'Em, in which each spouse or spouse-to-be throws back a few people from the couples' joint hand. The goal, in theory, was to arrive at a culled, combined social set both partners could live with. But Texas Hold 'Em served the joint purpose of commanding and proving loyalty, demonstrating that the future spouse was indeed most important and that anything or anybody that interfered too heavily with that relationship would be tossed aside.

Dan picked my friend Monique, who'd moved from Chicago to San Francisco about the same time I did, to complete an emergency medicine residency at Highland Hospital. Monique, like Dan, was very conventionally good-looking—blue eyes, blond hair, smile like a half moon. Like Dan, she was also intense, possessive, smart, and pedantic. Plus they both made themselves impossible to stand when we were all together, fighting ruthlessly over trivial matters like how best to exit the Kabuki Shopping Center parking garage. Dan maintained that one could stop to pay the attendant in the spot labeled "Five Minute Parking." Monique insisted that this was rude. Or maybe it was the other way around—who could care? The only relevant point is that they couldn't tolerate each other and didn't want to be together. I planned to marry one and not the other. I felt I had to choose. Still, the peremptory process was dreadful.

For a few weeks, I thought I might just weasel out—not return Monique's phone calls, fail to make dates. But she was too self-respecting for that, so we met at Que Tal, a café on Guerrero Street, to break up. Later, I realized the obvious: I should have pursued the friendship separately. But early on I lacked the sophistication and confidence to cultivate an independent self. As a result our split was gruesome, a Neil LaBute play—milky coffee going cold in glass mugs, Monique's direct question: "Are we going to be friends in the future or not?"

"I don't know, Monique," I said.

"It seems like you do know, so why don't you answer the question?"

Finally, wincing, I said no. Now I wish I'd said yes. For starters, Monique is great and I allowed myself to be swayed by Dan in a way I now wish I'd resisted.

Also, that coffee wasn't the end.

About six years later, after both Hannah and Audrey had been born, I ate some crab. It turned out I'm allergic to crab, but I didn't know that yet. So in the middle of the night I woke up, expelled crab, as Dan likes to tell the story, "from both ends," screamed "Da—," then blacked out and smacked my head on the bathroom floor. Dan ran in, alarmed—or so he tells me. I had passed out. He picked me up, slapped my face, tried some CPR. Then, convinced I was dying, he called 911.

By the time the ambulance arrived I'd brushed my teeth and put on the good men's-cut pajamas Dan had bought me when I was pregnant with Hannah. Dan needed to stay home with the girls, so the EMTs whisked me alone off to the hospital, and as I lay in one of those emergency room cubes so egregiously characterless they make you wonder if you really are dead, in walked the on-call doctor: Monique. She indulged herself just a single crack: Dan must really be lousy at CPR; my ribs weren't even bruised. Then she sat on the end of the hospital bed, offering me some of the homemade cookies she'd brought to help pass the night. In the morning I took a cab home and fell into bed. Hannah and Audrey never knew I'd left.

A year or two after that, Dan and Monique began bumping into each other at the Ferry Plaza farmer's market, a place I refused to go on account of the four-dollar-a-pound pears. There Monique and Dan discovered in each other fellow fanatics about the much-overlooked brilliance of master contrarian and science writer, *Good Calories, Bad Calories* author Gary Taubes. By that point Monique had married a Jewish lawyer and had a child of her own. Texas Hold 'Em was over, but I still felt a pang every time I saw Monique—felt reminded of the ways I'd failed in marriage early on. I hadn't failed Dan or let him down. I'd failed to value enough the parts of my life outside of Dan. I'd failed myself.

Not surprisingly, when Dan and I drove back over the Golden Gate for our second and final eight-hour installment of Mastering the Mysteries of Love, it was not all trapdoors opening in the heart. Since our last session, the Marin Headlands had greened up under the clear blue skies, but the *Days of Heaven* couple looked even more haggard than before, his hair more wild, her eyes primed with tears.

Keith, our instructor, collected us again around his dining room table.

"So, how'd your weeks go?" he asked in his nice British accent.

"Great," Dan said, eager as a child to give the right answer in class.

The *Days of Heaven* husband picked his head up off the table. He said, "We failed miserably." Then he dropped his head again.

Our task that day was to move past venting our disagreements toward solving them, too. Given the glorious weather, Dan and I claimed

Keith's back deck, where we sat atop his covered hot tub, in the dappled sunshine, warming up on such trivial matters as the brown socks Dan left strewn around the house. Inexorably, though, we circled back to our fight over how to spend summer weekends, that magnet of conflict that pulled us for reasons we did not yet understand. Only this time we realized within a few angry minutes that our failure to solve it was not due to a lazy lack of empathy. We actively maintained the distance between us. I would not join Dan in his bitter, hyperbolic characterization of my parents and their home. Yes, my mother was a neat freak and oversensitive to Dan's messes. But Dan *chose* to make those messes, and I thought my mother tried in her way. It just wasn't enough. Dan often returned from encounters with my family saying he felt like "a space alien." I felt this, too, at times; the feeling propelled me toward Dan. Still, I didn't blame my mother alone for the conflict between her and my husband. I thought it was ancient and inevitable. Dan took this stance as traitorous. We both felt angry and stuck.

"In most of life," Dan started out, inching backward to keep his face in the shade of a tall pine, "we have this give and take. We balance each other's needs. But then we hit this thing"—my desire to go to Napa, which Dan hated; my sense of filial duty—"and your mother's needs win. One hundred percent, without a doubt, no questions asked. You and the kids are going whether I like it or not, no discussion, boom, done. It's like I'm cut out of the family. And on top of that—on top of feeling excluded from the family, like I don't actually *have* a family—there's the very real issue of all the other things we *don't* do."

"We're not supposed to use inflammatory language," I said curtly. "Can you just express your feelings without screaming at me?"

Dan's core problem was this: because of my my-way-or-the-highway attitude—taking the girls to my parents' regardless of his feelings about it and shutting down conversation with the false concession that he could tag along if he so chose—we didn't expose the girls to *his* California: the secret camping spots in Yosemite Valley, the tide pools on the coast. Dan knew the names of a hundred wildflowers in Tuolumne Meadows. He knew which climbing routes had beautiful granite and which had loose rocks. Not passing this along to our girls felt like cauterizing part of his lineage.

I buttoned my jeans jacket over my tank top and folded my knees under my skirt. I loved that Dan knew these things. I'd spent the best summer of my life working as a student ranger at Black Canyon in Colorado. I wanted to be married to an ontologist of dudedom, a man in touch with the natural world. I also knew that Silverado, my parents' golf community, had bulldozed and turned under everything wild within its borders. But I felt devoted to my parents. They'd both spent their entire adult lives far away from their own parents, which I suspected they both regretted, at least once their mothers were widowed. I wouldn't have chosen Silverado. I bridled at the conventionality, the neighbors who installed double-paned windows so they would not hear my children playing in the street. But I wanted my parents to know my children as I had not known my grandparents. Besides, we did show the girls the mountains. We spent at least a week every summer in the Sierra together with the Duanes.

Above us, in an oak tree, we heard the desperate cries of a baby squirrel. I also felt myself falling into a rhetorical crevice. The further we bore down into this conversation, the more I felt my sense of duty toward my parents pitted against my sense of duty toward Dan. I hated this, the bedrock pain of marriage, the one hinted at by the tears falling as a father walks his daughter down the aisle (though we often tell ourselves these are tears of joy): You leave your own family. You form another with your spouse. And that new family, by definition, is a compromise.

"So you feel like my primary allegiance is to my mom sometimes, and that makes you question my love?" I heard myself saying in the fading afternoon light. Dan and I often spent twenty-one hours a day together. When my mother called I often didn't answer the phone. The class was doing its job, forcing Dan and me to confront the real issues of marriage (control, devotion, unity, autonomy) instead of chasing each other's tails around a thicket of logistics. Still I didn't want to see my love for my parents in opposition to my love for my husband. Yet, in some ways, it was.

8

Family

The most effective seventy-three seconds I dedicated to improving my marriage were those I spent watching a web video by Nick Sanabria called *Third Race at the Honeymoon Is Over Downs.* It starts with a series of thoroughbreds entering the gates.

"They're out of the gate, and they're off," the announcer calls, as if at the Preakness. "Jumping out in the lead is Romance and Affection, with Domestic Bliss in close behind. It's Romance and Affection and Domestic Bliss. . . . Here comes Marriage Vows followed by Immediate Child. Romance and Affection falling off quickly. Mortgaged up the Ass overtaking Domestic Bliss. . . . And here comes Nasty Attitude, followed by More Children and Drinking Heavily." By mid-race it's "I Don't Give a Shit taking the lead, followed by the Fucking House, You Cook Like Shit, and I Fucked Your Brother. . . . Here they come spinning out of the turn. I Don't Give a Shit still in front. Up Yours Keith challenging for the lead. Up Yours Keith and I Don't Give a Shit neck and neck. And down the stretch they come. . . . Up Yours Keith is pulling away from I Don't Give a Shit by a length. Coming on strong is I

Am Outta Here, and passing the pack is the Fucking House. And at the wire it's Up Yours Keith, the Fucking House, I Don't Give a Shit, and I Am Outta Here."

I loved this—totally loved it, which was surprising, even instructive, given that until I'd watched the video, one of the things I'd been most reluctant to change about my marriage was my delusion that it was entirely unique. Embarrassingly enough, I'd maintained the fantasy that my *whole life* was unique until I found myself screaming on my hands and knees in labor at the Kaiser San Francisco hospital, feeling intense kinship with a woman in Mozambique I'd read about. During a flood, she'd delivered her daughter in a tree. She and I were sisters (at least according to me), two humans giving birth. As a mother, I welcomed knowing that the most important thing in my life was also the most banal. But this sentiment did not extend to my marriage. My marriage was supposed to be special, sui generis. Cookie-cutter marriages—Stepford marriages—were creepy and for dopes.

Then came the mortal blow to this indulgence: an Imago therapy workshop in San Ramon. Imago therapy was created by Harville Hendrix, author of *Getting the Love You Want,* and I chose the workshop because I thought it might help me understand the fight Dan and I kept having about Napa. Imago therapy focuses on how our relationships with our parents and our baggage from childhood influence our marriages. It starts from three assumptions. One, we're all born whole. Two, we're all damaged by our parents. And three, we're all looking in romantic love for stand-ins for our parents (what Hendrix calls *imagos*), people who share our mothers' and fathers' strengths and weaknesses, thus can help us repair our childhood wounds.

Dan skipped—improvement fatigue—so it was just six other couples and I listening as Mindy McHugh, coproprietor of the One Relationship at a Time therapy practice, whispered to us through a cordless microphone in her suburban town house–like office suite.

"Close your eyes, relax your body, breathe through your belly. Now you're thirty years old, now you're twenty-five, now you're twenty, now you're fifteen, now you're ten, now you're five. . . ."

On the walls of One Relationship at a Time, which Mindy shared with a therapist named Ralph, hung half a dozen photographs of bridges—covered bridges, suspension bridges—each meant to remind clients that to reach another person's heart, you need to build an emotional span from yours to theirs. But Mindy didn't begin our day by focusing on bridges or connections with other people. She began by backing each of us deep into ourselves.

"You're in a warm safe space, filled with light."

And there I was in my Speedo, with my bowl-cut hair, lying on a towel next to the Wightman Tennis Center swimming pool. My mother dropped me off on hot weekend days and during summer vacations. The cement under my towel felt prickly and warm. The air smelled of cut grass and chlorine.

"Now invite your mother, or your mother-like caretaker, to the edge of your safe space. . . ."

And there she is, not in her one-piece swimsuit with the huge molded cups (why did she wear such matronly swimsuits? She had a pinup's figure) but in her street clothes: brown loafers with no socks, brown-and-orange chevron-striped pants, brown turtleneck and bouffant hairdo. She's standing, happy but rushed—her usual mode—eager to race off to the grocery store and Captain Marden's fish market to buy the ingredients to make the dinner my father had posted on the bulletin board. Each Sunday night my father tacked up a week's worth of menus, complete with cookbooks and page numbers. Amazingly, my mother then followed the plan.

"Now say good-bye to your mother, let her drift away, and invite your father or your father-like caretaker to the edge of your safe space."

And, boom, there he is, too, like the apparition of Jodie Foster's dead father in the Carl Sagan movie *Contact,* only in fantastically preppy clothes. I stare at my father, in his blue poplin pants with the red embroidered lobsters, and he stares back. He's warm, smart, and gentle, but I've frozen him out. I don't feel known or understood. I appreciate that he loves me, but I feel scared that he loves me *too* much, that I don't deserve it, that his love is based on a fantasy. I also feel ashamed that I'm not very nice to him. I've been pushing my father hard—ignoring questions, slamming doors, leaving rooms—in hopes that he'll get angry and demand I give him his due respect. But this is not his nature. "Judy, don't yell at me!" he snaps at the first hint of displeasure in my mother's voice. I don't like being so unpleasant to my father, but I don't know how to stop, either.

I'd long balked at the idea that I would settle into a marriage like my parents. Especially when I was younger and I viewed them in black and white: mom good, dad bad, simple as that. This reductive view paired poorly with a second habit of my juvenile mind: a tendency to take a little knowledge and stretch it, with total confidence, way too far. This started on the day I came home from Schofield Middle School and announced to my mother that she was an alcoholic because she had a glass of wine every night. I'd learned in health class that daily drinking was bad, especially drinking alone, and my mom poured herself six ounces of Chardonnay even on the nights my father traveled for business and her dinner consisted of half a bag of Doritos, consumed while reading the *Boston Globe* on the couch.

Later my penchant for stretching my limited and decontextualized knowledge ad adsurdum became more accusatory still. In my early teens I learned—again at school, this time sex ed—that relationships were supposed to be fun. Had my parents been having fun lately? I thought not. I decided to ask point-blank "Where's the fun, Mom?" during what I later learned was the worst year of my parents' marriage. My father worked in real estate finance. In the late 1980s he had a deal "go bad," a deal that became known in our house by the shorthand "Kansas City." Because of Kansas City, my father had some serious financial stress. No fun at all. Of course, neither of my parents explained Kansas City to me.

They maintained, well into my thirties, that one did not discuss money around the kids. All I knew was that the fun was gone. I fed this into the wood chipper of my teenage brain: mom good, dad bad; no more fun. Why was my mother still married to him?

My Imago instructor Mindy did not subscribe to the idea that our marriages are our own creations. She subscribed instead to the poet Philip Larkin's "They fuck you up, your mum and dad" school of thought. To make this absolutely clear, after whispering us out of our safe spaces and back to the present, she played a few scenes from the movie *The Prince of Tides*: Henry Wingo screaming at his beautiful wife as his children scatter toward the South Carolina coast; one of the same children, grown, walking on the beach, fighting with his own spouse. Mindy encouraged us to parse this neatly: screwed-up beach-dwelling father, screwed-up beach-dwelling son. Then she sent us outside to complete six pages of charts: five detailing what we loved and hated as children about our parents, how they'd made us feel incomplete or whole; then a sixth page on which we used our previous responses to complete a psycho-marital MadLibs.

My unconscious agenda was to get my caretakers who were sometimes (items circled on page 17)[*] with whom I often felt (items circled on page 23, #2)[†] because they often frustrated me by (items *underlined* and circled on page 21, #1)[‡] which made me fear (items circled on page 23, #3)[§] to always b (items *underlined* on page 17)[¶] instead of (page 24, #1)[**] so that I could have experienced (page 23, #4)[††] and always felt (items circled on page 19, #2)[‡‡]. . . .

---

[*]   tense, rushed
[†]   misunderstood, hurried
[‡]   not listening and not apprehending who I really was
[§]   being trampled or smothered
[¶]   loving and competent
[**]   tense, rushed, and not listening
[††]   feeling relaxed and known
[‡‡]   loved, energetic, encouraged, and approved

And there was my psyche, exposed as in an adolescent game of truth-or-dare: My parents made me feel hurried and unknown. Dan was a master of lingering and tuning in.

Before Dan I'd had a few boyfriends who seemed to be the kind of people I should marry and a few who did not. The ones who appeared to be right came first. Andy: my WASPy-yet-menschy high school boyfriend, who started me on my lifelong habit of being a nerdy girl attached to a cooler guy. Then Dave, my college boyfriend, who conducted his social life based on the philosophy that if it's not funny the first time, say it again. I was a serial monogamist. I met Dave my junior year at Yale. We'd both signed up for a class called Wilderness in the North American Imagination, a seminar for which we read books by John Muir and Clarence Scott King, books Dan later noted approvingly on my shelves. Dave, like my father, was Jewish, devoted to his mother and unburdened by artistic visions of any kind. He prepped at Choate and captained the swim team. His main creative outlet was being a ham. While dating him I bought my first car, a used Volkswagen Scirocco (probably because my parents, as Jews of a certain age, refused to drive German cars), and to celebrate Dave made me a mixed tape on which he sang the Eagles' "Hotel California" horribly, a cappella, by himself. Dave graduated a year before I did, and I thought I loved him. So when I finished college I joined Dave in Chicago, where he worked—to his great joy—as the brand manager for the cereal Honey Bunches of Oats. But once in Chicago I realized that I wasn't in love. I knew this because, when I began looking for my own apartment, I refused to live near Dave, in Lincoln Park. My own apartment needed to be farther from the lake.

Not because I didn't like the lake—the lake was fantastic. I insisted on being far from the lake because according to Chicago's social geography, at least how I perceived it, living near the lake meant "staying on the bus," and staying on the bus was my own personal shorthand for adhering to the route mapped out by my folks. That route entailed moving from one's preppy suburban childhood home to one's fancy college; detouring briefly, post-college, through an upscale urban neighborhood, like Lincoln Park. Then marrying and speeding back to the suburbs.

The boyfriends who seemed like the wrong kinds of people for me to marry were indeed the wrong kinds of people for me to marry, and even I knew this at the time. But they did grab the pull cord and yank me off the bus. Shane drove a toylike blue Miata convertible, with the top down, heat blasting, year round. I fell phenomenally in love with Shane. He was deft as a puppy at culling affection; needy and playful, he relished minor irresponsibilities: spur-of-the-moment road trips, spending too much. Within a few months, Shane had convinced me to quit my job as a textbook editor so I could jerk lattes at a coffee shop and try to write. I knew zero adults who'd made career decisions like this. During our four years together we each moved constantly: Shane to New York, I to Cambridge, both of us to Cape Cod. Then we returned together to Chicago, to an apartment on Logan Boulevard, far from the lake. But soon the fact that I didn't want to marry Shane started to bother me. I was twenty-seven. He gave me a plant for my birthday. I failed to water it while he was on a road trip. We broke up.

Until Dan, I never thought I'd marry any of my boyfriends, and as far as I know, none of them ever imagined they'd marry me. This always struck me as clear-sighted and sane. Why force that dream? But with Dan I felt different. Yes, we met when I was pushing thirty years old, marrying age—not inconsequential. But I always felt Dan was "right." Even the picture on the back of his book, *Caught Inside,* looked right to me. Dan was manly, not boyish; handsome but flawed. He was pedantic, sensitive, and he lost his temper. But he was passionate. He was smart. He listened to me. Life was not a bore. Perhaps most important, he gave me the lover's gift Stendhal describes in *On Love*: Dan saw me as beautiful, and that helped me see beauty in myself.

One warm afternoon, in my perfect-for-one Dorland Street apartment, Dan and I made love, then lay in the jasmine-scented air discussing the ideal rhythm for our days: write, work out, sex, dinner, watch a movie or read, sleep. I stood to pull on my clothes, then cook for Dan what he would now surely consider an inedible stir-fry: boneless skinless chicken breast, broccoli, water chestnuts, scallions, Hoisin sauce. Dan clasped his freckled hands behind his head, watching me dress. "I've never met anyone even a little bit like you," he said.

I burst out laughing. "Have you not met yourself?"

This feeling of deep familiarity I had with Dan: Did it matter? Was it good? Most of the world has discounted love, let alone the idea of a soul mate, when selecting a spouse. Nearly every historical or anthropological book about marriage makes this point: Stephanie Coontz, the country's foremost marriage historian, does so right in her subtitle to *Marriage, a History*: *How Love Conquered Marriage*. Elizabeth Gilbert, in *Committed*, when she asks a group of Hmong women their "secret to a happy marriage," admits that her culturally oblivious question cracks them up. Even Lori Gottlieb, in *Marry Him! The Case for Settling for Mr. Good Enough*, encourages contemporary American women to abandon the search for Mr. Right. "My advice is this: Settle!" she writes partway through a tract she describes as "like those graphic anti–drunk driving public service announcements that show people crashing into poles and getting killed," except her warnings are intended for single aging women. "That's right. Don't worry about passion or intense connection. Don't nix a guy based on his annoying habit of yelling 'Bravo!' in movie theaters. . . ." According to Gottlieb, seeking a perfect match is not just a low-odds game; it's a fool's errand. The higher your hopes rise on the sine curve of life, the greater the trough of disillusionment into which you will fall.

After the lunch break at the Imago workshop, Mindy, again with her cordless microphone, guided us through another role-playing exercise. In it, each couple pairs off. One spouse plays him- or herself as a child.

The other plays that child's opposite-sex parent. The two then have an encounter session.

I felt very relieved that Dan had stayed home. I didn't want to pretend to be his mother, Kit, nor did I want Dan to mimic my dad. Throughout my life, friends had tried to imitate him—blinking slowly, mumbling—and despite my own issues with my father, I'd always felt protective and annoyed. Shane alone took a generous tack: He decided that my father was a comic genius, more deadpan than Steven Wright, and that my mother was the ultimate straight man, the only one in on the joke. Mindy called for volunteers to model the role-playing exercise. Up stepped a woman with short hair and her husband, in a pressed white snap-button shirt. Earlier that morning, on a break, the two had told me that they'd packed their kite boards in their car, so if the workshop was terrible, they'd be able to salvage their day. I related intensely, my running shoes in the trunk. Now, the kite-boarding couple pulled two chairs into the semicircle formed by the group.

"How old are you?" Mindy asked the woman.

"Fourteen," she said.

Her husband's eyes widened. Mindy nodded for them to start.

Husband (as wife's father): I'm your father. What's it like living with me?

Wife (as self, age fourteen): I don't live with you. You live in Brazil.

Husband: What do you need me to know about your life?

Wife: I need you to know that I'm sleeping with the man across the street who is the father of three. I didn't initiate it. You weren't here to protect me. I feel vulnerable and afraid.

Husband: You feel vulnerable and afraid.

Wife: Yes.

Husband: That makes sense, I wasn't here to protect you, so when the man across the street suggested that you two start sleeping together, you didn't feel I was there to protect you.

Wife: Yes.

I couldn't take it anymore. I decided to leave. This felt too voyeuristic, especially without my own spouse. But as all the other couples paired off, Mindy's therapy partner, Ralph, approached me. "Is it international take-a-risk day?" he asked.

"I'm not sure what you mean."

"I mean, would you be willing to do the role-play, with me sitting in for your husband as your father?"

I started to sweat even before we sat down. I looked at Ralph, this man I didn't know. Imagining he was Dan pretending to be my father produced a sick vertigo. But I slowed my breathing, then reeled back my mind to when I was sixteen. It was after dinner and must have been summer because the sky was still light. I was up in my bedroom with the periwinkle rug that matched the periwinkle curtains, Laura Ashley duvet (so much Laura Ashley), the built-in dresser with the mirror above, topped by six exposed spherical bulbs as if this were a dressing room at a cabaret show. As I told Ralph, I'd fled the dinner table because I couldn't stand being around my dad. I was angry with him for asking, again, if there was much school spirit. I was angry with him for seeming so solicitous of me, for wanting me to be an extension of himself. I felt bored with school, desperate to move on, uninspired by the dreams set forth for me but not yet in possession of my own. I told Ralph, as my father, that I felt aggrieved that he, my dad, was not the father I wanted him to be. He was not cool. He was not tough. I knew that he was proud of me, but he did not seem to know who I was. So, what was he so proud of? Something real? Something true? I'd also retreated to my room because I didn't want to eat with my parents. I thought my parents used food as a proxy for closeness. I thought they lacquered over emotion with place mats and ritual. Every birthday, every graduation, every turning point worth noting, was celebrated by a formal hours-long meal on the theory—really, the superstition—that if we all sat down together with a tuna tartare and an efficient waiter all must be in order. But all was not in order, not with me. I was growing anxious and queasy on the bus. In my late teens, I knew I didn't want the life set out for me, but I didn't yet know anything else.

When I opened my eyes I felt as if I should have said something worse. I'd never done enough therapy to understand completely my relationship with my parents. Even in recovering from anorexia, I'd resisted digging too deep. The idea that my eating disorder was my parents' fault felt accusatory and diminishing. It was my problem; I'd caused it. I didn't want to pin my pathology on my mother and father. Relative to marriage improvement, I also felt protective of my parents. Unlike Dan, they had not consented to a year of poking at the underbrush of our relationship and publishing the results. I worried doing so would not go well. I knew what I voiced to Ralph did not constitute a very impressive family drama. But my parents made reasonable requests from me, did they not? Shouldn't I just give them what they wanted?

"Is that all for today?" Ralph asked.

My blouse soaked through, I said yes. I felt frantic to see Dan. During the last nine years I had come to realize he was not exactly the person I thought I had wed. He was less drifty, more obsessive and tortured; also, in his own ways, more different from me. He liked rules. He was stealthily conservative. These offsets were good—we could have benefited from more. But Dan gave me what I needed most: He knew who I was. I used to joke that this was the reason people marry: to have someone who can observe your family at close enough range to help you figure out who you and they are.

I remained at the workshop nearly to the end, until the holding exercise. Then as everyone else lay on the floor cuddled in pairs envisioning a state of perfect connection—each partner a lock; his mate, the key—I drove toward the Caldecott Tunnel, hoping to arrive home in time to change my clothes before meeting Dan and my parents at a restaurant called Spruce to celebrate my father's seventy-second birthday. But traffic was snarled. I called Dan and asked him to bring me a clean dress, then drove straight there.

Spruce was the kind of restaurant I couldn't stand when I was younger: a "big occasion" restaurant, with heavy chairs and pretentious-sounding entrées like "Rabbit in Three Preparations with Chantenay Carrots and Umbrian Lentils." My mother was standing out front when I walked up. She'd been living in California three years by then, and she'd never looked more beautiful—great hair, sleek clothes.

"I can't believe I'm still going to dinners like this," I said, hugging her as my father parked their car.

"You know we're eating here because of Dan," my mother said with a laugh. Dan had started curing pancetta in our basement. "We thought he'd enjoy the salumi."

9
Food

"Honey, I have to tell you something," Dan said to me a few years earlier, after setting a bowl of homemade turnip and turnip greens soup with fresh croutons on my desk for lunch. "I bought a whole lamb today. It's a really good lamb, grass fed, organic. And I promise I won't tyrannize you with it. I just got a great price on it, and it's the same kind of lamb they serve at Chez Panisse. . . ."

Then he sat there staring at me.

At that point, we had thirty-five pounds of cow and fourteen pounds of deer in our basement freezer. We also had some duck breast prosciutto curing in the refrigerator and a heritage pork belly dangling above the washer-dryer. It was blue with mold.

When Dan and I first met he made himself exactly one serving of pasta each night. It consisted, regardless of season, of one quarter of a bell pepper, half a red onion, half a tomato, and four or five cloves of garlic, which Dan now recognizes he browned until bitter. And his cooking remained more or less at that level—in fact, we shared the cooking—until Hannah was born. Then we started having the same conversation every night: Do you want to cook or look after the kid? Dan always picked cook, I always picked kid. So in his extremely male, obsessive way, he decided if he was going to cook, he might as well acquire some skills.

I should have been scared—Dan does not take skill-acquisition lightly. He'd lived out of his truck in Yosemite for three summers so he could learn to climb big walls. He chose the literature Ph.D. program at U.C. Santa Cruz based on its proximity to good surf. The flamenco guitar obsession (immediately preceding the cooking obsession, when I was pregnant and Dan began realizing our life would require more time at home) is painful to remember. Dan grew out and shellacked his nails. The vocals sounded like primal screams. With the cooking I did notice, during Hannah's infancy, that Dan was trying to perfect his tofu-frying technique with a level of twitchy mania I'd only ever seen in a pyromaniac mixing homemade rocket propellant in the Mojave Desert. ("Here I go with my bad self, adding potassium nitrate!") But at least Dan's efforts led to dinner.

As I now know, we were slogging through that high-risk patch called "transition to parenthood." Experts used to claim that children guaranteed a happy marriage. (A deluded editor at *Better Homes and Gardens* wrote, in 1944, once a child arrives "we don't worry about this couple anymore.") But then the war and the 1950s ended, and since that time not a single peer-reviewed study has found that children make married couples happy. Actually, one study did. But then researchers found a coding error and issued an erratum.

Psychoanalysts offer many theories, including new fathers becoming enraged at both their infants and their wives, as the child has caused the wife to go AWOL from her previous post as the husband's mother-replacement figure. (This builds on another psychoanalytical doozy: that marriage is the most intense emotional relationship anybody has after babyhood, and as such it enables us to get back in touch with our infant selves.) But really it's simple: Caring for young children is stressful, and not very fun. Nobel Prize–winning economist Daniel Kahneman surveyed 909 working women in Texas. In terms of pleasurability, child care ranked sixteenth, out of nineteen activities, below even housework. In another study, researchers at UCLA shot 1,500 hours of video, recording daily life in two-income Los Angeles homes with at least two children. The postdoc who logged the tape described the experience as "the very purest form of birth control ever devised. Ever."

But during our transition to parenthood, I understood none of this. I just thought, while massively sleep deprived, that Dan was being an ass. I was stuck in the moment—the second, really (bursting into tears when Dan arrived home to relieve me of my parenting duties at 4:32 instead of 4:30). So I was not fully cognizant that, with tiny Hannah in the Bjorn, we were still laying the foundation of our civilization together. Nor did I pause to consider the direction that civilization was headed—toward a culinary dictatorship in the form of a one-table hobby restaurant at which all subjects ate at the mercy of the manic husband-chef—when Dan decided to cook every single recipe published by his former preschool teacher, Alice Waters of Chez Panisse.

During the Alice phase, which lasted three years, through the lost pregnancy and Audrey's birth, our house was filled with secrecy. Back then we wrote in side-by-side non-soundproofed offices, with a door in between them that didn't really close, so secrecy was hard to come by. But at least once an hour Dan would bolt from his desk up to the kitchen to, as he put it, "bust some moves." The moves involved feverishly skimming foam from a pot of chicken stock, or mincing shallots, or parboiling and shelling fava beans, or taking some incredibly expensive piece of meat out of the refrigerator and lacing it up with kitchen twine and putting it in a roasting pan. When I'd go upstairs to use the bathroom or make myself some tea, I'd find my surfer-dude husband hunkered over a cookbook wearing an apron. At our wedding, the one vow we'd rewritten for ourselves was "I promise to take you to be no other than yourself, loving what I know of you, trusting what I do not yet know." That trusting-what-I-do-not-yet-know part was now making me nervous. Up in the kitchen in the middle of the day, I'd try to pretend all this furtive cooking didn't freak me out. I'd strain to mutter something normal like, "What's for dinner, honey?"

Dan would say, "Oh, nothing, just some stuff."

Seven hours later, we'd sit down at the table to—I kid you not—nothing but a gigantic dish of the most beautiful onion gratin you'd ever seen, or a meal like the one that has come to be known in our house as "cardoons five ways," consisting of cardoon and artichoke ragout, bagna cauda, cardoon gratin, cardoon fritters, and cardoons à la grecque. (In case you didn't know—and I didn't—a cardoon is basically a celery stalk from the Jurassic era.)

Male obsession, even when it's not with another woman, has a way of making a wife feel cold. And so it was with Dan's first conquest, *Chez Panisse Vegetables,* a 344-page tome consisting of 290 recipes, organized by vegetables (amaranth greens, artichokes, asparagus, avocado, beans, beets and beet greens, broccoli and broccoli rabe, etc.).

I know, it sounds extremely pleasant to be on the receiving end of such a project. Lord knows it sounded this way to all of my girlfriends, and pretty much everybody else who knew about it, and in hindsight it sort of was. But all those people were not me. They hadn't grown up feeling smothered and disregarded by the focus on food and the endless restaurants. Nor were they left alone to babysit the chef's frantic children while all this cooking was happening, nor did they understand that Dan's cooking was being driven by an individualistic desire to complete recipes and put little check marks next to them in the cookbook's table of contents, not by a desire to please his eaters. I also knew that Dan's cooking, and his obsessions in general, were mechanisms to bind anxiety, attempts to bring order to an unruly mind. In his early twenties, before we'd met, he'd learned the trick of focusing and applying himself at nearly all times. I respected this, even appreciated it. But I struggled, as I imagine all obsessives' spouses do, with the specifics.

A few warnings had flared in the run-up to our wedding, but I was so blinded by the miracle of Dan—his eyes, the smell of neoprene—that I hardly paid attention. For instance, I assumed we didn't care about the food at our reception. My parents' standards so far exceeded our own, I saw no point in getting involved. Especially with the cake. I didn't even want a cake. I wanted a wedding cobbler. So I declined, for both Dan and myself, the invitation to join my parents as they pinballed around Sonoma and Marin, visiting caterers and pâtissiers. One Saturday they called from Perfect Endings, reporting they'd signed a baker.

"You'll be happy," my mom announced from the baker's phone. "The cakes are not froufrou. He'll garnish with whole fruit. I just need to know what kind of cake you want."

I yelled out to Dan, across our apartment, "We don't care about the cake, right, honey?"

"Of course we care about the cake!"

"We do?"

"Of course we do. Give me the phone."

Dan grabbed the earpiece. My mom handed him off to the baker, who cut right to business: "How lemony?"

"Really lemony," Dan said.

"*Really* lemony?"

"Yes, really *really* lemony."

The baker explained the situation: He could easily make a really *really* lemony butter-cream frosting and really *really* lemony lemon curd filling, but to make the cake itself really *really* lemony, well, that would require artificial flavor and here Dan drew the line. At our nuptials, in Olema, Dan inhaled three servings of rack of lamb. Then, after serving the first slice of cake to me, he offered my father the second.

"That's all right, I don't like lemon," my father said, passing the plate along to my mom.

Dan swiveled his head back to me. "How did you let me do this?" he whispered.

"I didn't care about the cake."

Still I did not see Dan's cooking obsession coming, and a small rift started to form between us early on, after Dan made a salad of curly endive and persimmons that I absolutely adored. This was great, right? An opportunity for marital renewal? Not in my house. The attitude from the kitchen was onward and upward. Dan had 289 other recipes to attend to in *Chez Panisse Vegetables* alone, not to mention *Chez Panisse Café, Chez Panisse: Cooking, Chez Panisse Menu Cookbook, Chez Panisse Fruit,* and *Chez Panisse: Pasta, Pizza, Calzone.* My taste became irrelevant. We didn't eat that persimmon salad again for four years.

Another wrinkle: my praise of Dan's cooking, or lack of same.

While I had grown up in a relatively tight-lipped suburban home (my father's response to my mother's making veal scallopini, potato gratin, and garden salad on a Wednesday night was to mumble, "It's good"), Dan was raised lavishly adored. No event in his family was unsuitable for heaping on accolades. Dan's middle name is King—after the civil rights activist C. B. King, but still. His mother also regularly told Dan that he was an outstanding musician and songwriter and really should be a rock star, despite the fact that he's tone deaf and has no sense of rhythm. This was especially confusing for Dan, as at age twelve he started taking guitar lessons with his neighborhood friend, Charlie Hunter, who went on to have a great jazz recording career, while Dan's high school band, the Dark, folded after just one show, featuring "God Save the Queen" by the Sex Pistols. As a result, every time Dan served a meal, he sat across our wooden table waiting for a level of praise I was not only unwilling (he was not cooking for me, after all, was he?) but constitutionally unable to provide.

Nobody understood the trauma of this except Kelly, Dan's sister. At that point, 2003–2004, she was living in the flat below us, so she was uniquely privileged to understand the situation, including just how much praise Dan was accustomed to receiving. Once, before Dan's cooking madness had started, Kelly was eating dinner at our house—grilled chicken breasts, salad—when Dan started telling a story about a fellow climber he knew who decided to climb fourteen 14,000-foot peaks in fourteen days. Most of my friends kept fit: yoga, cycling, running. Dan's friends did strenuously macho things, like surfing mountainous waves at Mavericks or climbing El Capitan. But this was another level entirely. "Oh my god, his poor girlfriend must be exhausted!" was Kelly's initial reaction. "How could she possibly do enough cheerleading for that?"

A few years later Kelly met and married Mario. Mario really is one of the best things ever to happen to my marriage. Not only does he make Dan look like a kitchen moderate—Mario won't let Kelly boil water for coffee; he thinks she does it wrong. (I am allowed to boil the water for coffee, just not to pour it over the grounds, because we make coffee with a cone placed directly over a mug and I refuse to preheat the cup.) Mario will join Dan in eating a meal of pig's trotters and beef heart carpaccio, which, when Dan wrapped up *Chez Panisse Vegetables* and started focusing more on meat, turned out to be a huge relief.

One week, during the meat extravaganza, Dan made, on four consecutive weeknights, quail, blood sausages, rabbit, and pigeon, all consumed at the table with Hannah and Audrey, who was then only two and declared herself done with a meal by swiping her plate onto the floor.

"You mean he actually cooks pork?" a friend asked when I began confessing my trauma around the cooking of strange meats.

Pork? How about tripe?

I started looking forward to Dan's nights out when we didn't have to sit through an increasingly intense meal of something Dan wanted to cook that I didn't want to eat, and the girls and I sat at the kitchen island, peaceful and relaxed, splitting a box of Annie's mac 'n' cheese.

Just about this time, in what I assume was an attempt at marriage education, Dan saw an article in the newspaper, clipped it out, and put it on my desk. A marketing and psychology professor in Florida, wondering why her husband, also a marketing and psychology professor, seemed to do the exact opposite of what she wanted him to do, began studying reactance. Reactance describes that all-too-human habit of a person going to strange, often self-defeating lengths to maintain one's autonomy in social situations by resisting other people's desires. In the marriage literature, reactance is often linked to "engulfment anxiety," the fear of being subsumed by one's spouse. People with engulfment anxiety have what academics call an "ontological insecurity"—an essentially unstable mental state. They worry about losing their personal integrity, thus tend to feel defensive, claustrophobic, and embattled. And I have to confess this concept really spoke to me. I thought it explained many things, including my hatred of the Ferry Plaza Farmer's Market, that hot mess of food-obsessed humanity and four-dollars-per-pound pears that overtakes the San Francisco Embarcadero Saturday mornings and is the highlight of Dan's week.

At any rate, this husband-and-wife team of reactance researchers managed to join forces (ha!) and found that the more one person wanted another to do something—like, say, clean up or eat weird meat for dinner—the less the second person wanted to do it. As if to demonstrate, one day around this time, at the Whole Foods in San Francisco's South of Market district, Dan and I got into a very large and embarrassing fight over my total commitment to buying what Dan accurately described as a bag of multicolored precooked French fries, so desperate was my need to assert my right to purchase convenience food. Dan, meanwhile, stopped putting away anything, ever, and I am fairly sure, though I can't confirm, that he began changing his clothes several times daily, letting each outfit, splattered with cooking grease, fall on our bedroom floor. We had many conversations-slash-fights trying to remind each other that life would not be better if our family descended into eating junk food in total squalor. Still, pretty much nothing got put away. And few things made me happier—or Dan more annoyed—than my taking the girls down the block for horrible slices of pizza.

One of the last remaining recipes from the Chez Panisse books was for headcheese, a French terrine made by boiling pigs' feet and a pig's head in a pot to release all the gelatin and meat. The main reason for the delay on the recipe was not the lack of audience (though there was that, too). The problem was the difficulty of procuring the main ingredient—a five-pound pig's head—a rarity, given that all the butchers in town who carried pigs' heads, with whom Dan was now acquainted, generally had heads weighing upward of twenty pounds. Dan was still a few years away from buying entire pigs and cutting apart their craniums in our basement. So one evening I noticed a large plastic bag in our refrigerator; the next morning, a stockpot on our stove with half a pig snout sticking out. Dan by this point had gotten into the whole Michael Pollan responsible meat-eating thing: I love the pig, I honor the pig, therefore I eat the pig's entire body. Except in Dan's mind it had been perversely distorted into I love the pig, I honor the pig, I'd like to eat the pig's entire body, but, really, it's too damn big, so with the utmost respect I band-saw in half the pig's head.

Dan even grossed himself out during the making of the headcheese, or half-head cheese as it might more properly be called, peeling the half pig's face off with his fingers and chopping up its half snout. But he put on a good show. He added some of the cartilage to the terrine, as Alice had suggested "for crunch." He served the whole dish up on a beautiful Italian platter we'd received as a wedding gift. Our friends Kate and Jamie, excellent comfort-food cooks, had come over for dinner, unaware of the menu. When the shimmering translucent dish hit the table, Hannah—who at that point was earning her keep in the house by declaring her love of squab—asked "Is it plastic?" Jamie ate a few bites, then pronounced it "a glorious failure." The main customer for the headcheese was Audrey who, at age two, still ate everything. Though even Audrey, after her first serving, started requesting "other one cheese," by which she meant the Parmesan.

Following Alice came Thomas Keller, with (even I admit) delectable dishes like skirt steak with caramelized shallots and red wine jus. The recipes seemed reasonable at first glance. In fact they were cruelly Byzantine, packed with sub-recipes inside recipes like those Russian dolls, so what looked like a fairly simple preparation—one Dan could whip off during my late-afternoon playground run with the girls—upon closer inspection, at that point usually mid-recipe, involved the making of red wine jus (1.5 hours), which itself involved the preparing of veal stock (4–5 hours of near-constant skimming), which of course drove me around the bend. I just wanted to eat something, anything, and then slip into the bath with the kids. But instead, during the Keller phase while we ate loaf after loaf of bread dipped in olive oil to stem our hunger, Dan and I started having these cryptic conversations about pleasure. Why didn't I care more about hedonistic joys? Was I some kind of Puritan?

At first, I assumed the conversations were really about sex, or at least my lack of enthusiasm for French kissing. But in the end Dan claimed to be talking just about food, questioning how he could be married to someone who'd happily throw the steak on the grill and forget about the jus. When I was a teenager I'd read that the secret to marriage was finding a way to keep walking in more or less the same direction. I wasn't quite sure how to keep walking toward the jus, and I found Dan's insinuation that somehow *I'd* lost the course, that a total commitment to perfect veal stock was somehow part of our vows, so aggravating I boycotted his cooking for a while and lost a few pounds. But finally, five years into his food obsession, Dan took a new approach. He eased up on the check marks and the Keller, and even, temporarily, on exotic meats. He launched into a romantic mission to unearth just what, at the table, could make his wife happy.

I wasn't the easiest nut to crack. At first I thought Dan was more lost than ever, like some off the-deep-end baseball nut taking his wife to see one team after another, figuring she just hadn't seen the right players to turn her into a fan. But just like every couple needs to find its own vacation spot, we needed to find our cookbook, and *Lulu's Provençal Table,* written by Richard Olney, brought us out of our stalemate. Lulu Peyraud wasn't a restaurant cook looking to make a few dollars or widen her fame by sharing trade secrets devised to impress paying customers. She was a home cook aiming to please her loved ones, foremost her husband, Lucien, and it showed.

One of the first Lulu meals Dan made started with Lucien's Soup, which Lulu describes as "just the soup I fix for Lucien every evening when we're alone." He set it out in a yellow tureen along with a stack of crispy garlic toast. I could tell Dan was cooking for me, that the monomania had broken. Lucien's soup was just potatoes, carrots, and turnips in a rich chicken stock, but it was delicious and it was healing. As we sat together, staring out our window at the green knob of Bernal Hill and a small sliver of the San Francisco Bay beyond, I felt like we'd started to find our way back—back toward the moment when Dan and I stood on the sidewalk on Guerrero Street and promised, "Let's do everything together."

Now our whole team was assembled. Not much prior, Hannah had asked me where Audrey was before she was born. I said, somewhat lamely, that Audrey was floating around up in the sky.

"Before I was born," Hannah then asked, "were we floating around together?"

I said yes again. Hannah broke into a beatific, the-world-feels-whole smile. I did not tell her that I imagined a boy floating with them, a boy I still often apologized to for not helping land.

The mirage of that almost-child hovered over my marriage. Since the moment I learned I was pregnant with Audrey, I'd thrown my heart into loving her. I refused to keep wishing for a different baby. I could not have carried both. But Dan still ached for that son, and I walled myself off from his pain. It cut too deep; it felt like a betrayal. But somehow over Lucien's soup we began, tentatively, to move forward. We'd had a loss, and it was dreadful, and our ways of coping had pushed us apart, but now I could see that we'd get through it. This was our family, our imperfect, blessed, and hurting family, sitting at this table. Hannah and Audrey drained the broth from their bowls, then ran off to their rooms to cover each other with face paint. Few dinners have felt more grounding and unexpectedly romantic than that one, consumed with mismatched napkins at our butcher block, covered as it always was in those days, with stickers, glitter, and glue.

Predictably, a few months after discovering Lulu, Dan fell off the please-the-wife wagon and bought his first pig. As part of a magazine assignment, he'd had a chance to learn how to make salumi with the chef of Perbecco, a hot new restaurant in town and, Dan being who he is, he asked the chef to throw another hog into his next order. So one Friday afternoon our phone rang—"Pig's here!"—and that Sunday Dan drove downtown to the restaurant to butcher the animal himself.

He said he'd be back in a couple of hours. It turned out to be eight. At about five hours post-departure I was truly irate, positive, once again, that all this cooking was ruining my marriage. In my rage I even fantasized about looking for a different husband in whom I could truly trust what I did not yet know. But by the time Dan returned, my feelings had mellowed. He'd called many times in the final two hours, explaining he was trapped in Perbecco's subterranean cutting room with a large, bald

Swedish sous-chef with a goatee. It also didn't hurt that he returned home ready for triage, including indulging me in one of my ultimate fantasies: takeout sushi.

As Dan ran back out to his truck to unload the pig, I poured myself a glass of wine and put the girls in the tub.

A few minutes later, as I sat on a stool, I heard Audrey splash and ask, "Where's Dada?"

Hannah seized the moment to educate her little sister. "He's butchering another pig."

10
Religion

One afternoon in May of 2010, after packing and repacking his bag, searching for just the right T-shirt and weight-lifting shorts, Dan drove to his gym to meet his strength-training guru, Mark Rippetoe. Rip, as Dan called him, happened to be in town from Wichita Falls, Texas.

Encounters with charismatic leaders rarely go as planned. At World Gym, Rip coached Dan for four hours, and when they finished Dan drove his mentor to Incanto, a nose-to-tail eatery in Noe Valley known for pushing the limits of what humans will pay good money to ingest. There in the dining room, to express his gratitude, Dan ordered pig's trotters, salumi, tuna-heart pasta, mackerel, two pork chops, and a lamb shoulder. "That's a big move," the chef said, approaching the table. "Are you sure about that?"

"You bet," Dan said. He and Rip ate everything. Dan felt sick for a week.

As spring rolled toward summer during that year of marital improvement, I'd started growing impatient with my sequential attempts at betterment and my decision to throw everything out of the messy closet that was our life and try to put it back in a way that resembled an ad for the Container Store. Not everything fit, it never would—nor would I have wanted it to, though I didn't realize this yet. During a frantic, few weeks' stretch in May, with the help of our analyst Holly and others, I worked on teasing apart the obligations I felt toward my mother from my actual desires to be with her; accepting Dan's compliments without suspicion that I was being manipulated (yet still returning a compliment to him—tricky); demanding the girls remain quiet while Dan and I finished conversations. I also met with Rabbi Larry Kushner, a minor celebrity in Semitic circles, credited with converting David Mamet into an Orthodox Jew.

The rabbi part, arranged by my father, was a disaster.

Kushner and I met at a dingy café on Russian Hill. He did not look much like a rabbi to me. He looked like Dan's father, compact and fit, dressed in fleece, with a white beard. Kushner sat at a corner table, like a graduate student, working on his new novel. For unrelated reasons—a stalled magazine story—I was feeling thwarted, and my sense of treading water in life was only amplified by the fact that Kushner didn't offer any mystical rabbinic marriage wisdom.

"I do what we all do," he said, shrugging. "I refer couples in trouble to marriage counseling."

When I pressed for something related to faith, he slipped into tradition. "In Jewish marriage, in a bizarre way, love is not in play. Love is to marriage what a refund is to your income tax return. You cannot set love as your goal. If it shows up, great." Then he invoked *Fiddler on the Roof,* the part when Tevya asks Golde, his wife of twenty-five years, "Do you love me?" and Golde answers, "Do I *what*?"

So, wanting to make the most of this meeting, I slipped into journalist mode, fishing for better material, stumbling upon the problem of interfaith marriage. I laid out our basics: Dan and I were raising our children as they were—part Jewish, part Christian. Given that neither of us was devout, we'd turned over the girls' religious training to our parents. Jewish holidays we celebrated with mine, Christmas and Easter with Dan's. My folks, predictably, took their job very seriously: children's services at their temple on Rosh Hashanah and Yom Kippur; a monthly subscription to the PJ Library book club, with kids' titles like *Hanukkah at Valley Forge* and *You Never Heard of Sandy Koufax?!* Up until the day I met Kushner, I felt solid and calm about our system. I helped trim the Christmas tree. Dan read at the Passover Seder. We didn't argue or question much. Our children *were* part Jewish, part Christian. Who were we to tell them otherwise?

Hearing this, Kushner slowly stroked his beard. Then he asked, "Would you *like* your children to be Jewish?"

This was a deft question, probing into my desires, and in answering it I made a tactical error. I said, "Sure, I'd love that."

I meant *Sure, I'd love the girls to be Jewish* in the same way I'd love a lot of things. I'd love for them to be great athletes. I'd love not to worry about money. I'd love to have a long neck. I also believed, apart from the neck, that I could make any one of these things happen if I cared enough. But I didn't care enough—at least not now. So the desires remained idle. That felt okay to me. That felt like life.

Kushner forwarded a different view. "Well, there's going to be a shit storm," he said at our small table, quietly and with utter confidence. "I'm not working for your father here, I want you to know that. But you would never tell your children, 'Today you wear pants, tomorrow you wear a dress.' Children need to be told who they are."

Work for my father? That hadn't even occurred to me. My father had recently boasted that he was Kushner's second-best student. "You can choose to deal with it lovingly now," Kushner said. "Or wait until it really hits the fan later."

I felt ten years younger than I usually felt, and very confused. "Okay, wait. What about Dan's family? We're very close to them. They're a huge part of our life. They're not exactly devout, but I'm worried they'll feel alienated if . . ."

Kushner took control of the conversation. "What's more important, your children or Dan's parents?"

That was the bargain? Later I could not believe I hadn't challenged Kushner, demanded different terms. But I didn't, I just sat there, receptive, as Kushner suggested we dispatch the problem of Christmas (which we would no longer celebrate) by building a sukkah each autumn in our backyard.

A sukkah? As in a straw hut hung with harvest fruits? This would replace the girls' baking and decorating gingerbread houses with Dan's mother; the *Nutcracker* and *Nutcracker*–re-creation in our living room; the annual party at the Duanes at which Santa arrived, exhausted on the night of the twenty-fifth, his reindeer desperate for dog food? Kushner really believed that we could remove this beam from our family architecture and the structure would still stand? He had faith that a major rift was not going to form between Dan's parents and me when we informed them that our children's religious identities would not include them?

I felt outwitted, confused. All right, Sukkot, no Christmas. I supposed the girls would enjoy the exotic fruits if I could marshal the enthusiasm. Dan had once brought a citron home from the farmer's market; it looked like a lemon octopus, a thrill to the girls. Finally, to complete my self-immolation, I told Kushner I wanted the girls to *feel* Jewish. As I explained, I liked *feeling* Jewish myself. But I didn't want to send the girls to religious school.

Kushner didn't think much of this reasoning, either. "Have you ever seen the stained glass in Temple Sherith Israel?" he asked.

I shook my head no.

"It shows Moses with the Ten Commandments, on Half Dome. Half Dome! This isn't New York. Nobody just *feels* Jewish in California. You need to send them to religious school. You have to train them to be Jewish. That's how a person feels Jewish—you teach them Jewish ritual!"

At home I found Dan chopping asparagus stalks and artichoke hearts into tiny cubes for some absurdly complicated recipe from Le Bernardin. "Don't you want to hear about my day?" I asked, pulling a stool up to our kitchen island. "It was pretty weird."

"OK," Dan said, still chopping. I could hear in his voice that he already suspected my day had led me nowhere good. "How was your day?"

"Well, I sort of realized that I *do* care if the girls grow up Jewish. I think maybe it means a lot to me."

Dan set down the knife.

"I know this is not what we agreed originally, but the rabbi really thinks we need to deal with it now, instead of waiting around until the girls are twenty-five and not Jewish and I'm wondering how I let this happen."

Dan allowed this sentence to dangle for a moment.

Then he said, "You've got to be fucking kidding me."

I could hear Hannah and Audrey jumping on the trampoline next door, shrieking and bouncing with their friend Cuya, launching themselves toward the canopy of the brush box tree, occasionally smacking skulls. Their school year was winding down, their little bodies relaxing, their progress through another grade certified by the return of a ziplock bag filled with emergency school clothes that no longer fit. Then Dan exploded.

"Who the hell gave that guy the right to tell us how to raise our family? He meets you for twenty minutes, and he decides the best thing for us is to dump my family over the side and raise our kids as Jews? How can he even in good conscience say that? He doesn't give a shit about what's good for me or our kids or our marriage or even for you. He wants one thing: Jews. And everybody else can fuck themselves."

I tried to sit still, on the wooden stool at our kitchen island, letting this sink in. I did not like this aspect of Judaism, either. I liked the contentious, anti-didactic part, what Tony Judt called the "collective self-questioning . . . the awkwardness and dissent." I also realized, for the first time in our marriage project, I'd crossed an important line. I'd gone badly out of bounds. I'd confused the idea of working toward a better marriage—a decidedly joint proposition—with straining to grab more of what I wanted, or been convinced I wanted, for myself. You'd think, by then, that I would have settled this confusion, that I would have grown accustomed to the idea that Dan was a particular person with particular needs and that I had to account for those needs, always. I couldn't bluster or bullshit. I couldn't put things over on him. This was one of the most difficult parts of marriage for me: accepting Dan and his eternal specificity. He was never vague, nor was he optional, a convenience to take or leave as I wished. He was not an extension of myself. I sensed the core difficulty of this in my twenties, before I met Dan, when I memorized a line from one of Lorrie Moore's short stories. Marriage, Moore writes, is "a fine arrangement in general, except one never got it generally. One got it very, very specifically."

My specific husband was prickly and gentile. He did not want his edges rounded off. And despite this, I'd told a rabbi that I would love for my children to be Jewish. Then I'd allowed that rabbi to convince me I needed to act, to fight for what I wanted, irrespective of Dan.

"I don't want my daughters being told they are different from me in some fundamental way," Dan said after a few moments of silence.

"Oh, sweetie, I'm so sorry," I said. I knew he was right.

The question of what we were going to "do" about religion first arose ten years prior, as Dan and I were driving with my parents around northern California, looking at wedding venues. We'd just left the White House Inn (too informal for my mother, or, really, for my grandmother, who thought it was bad enough that we wanted to marry outside and not in a fancy hotel). Dan was winding my taxicab-yellow Volkswagen hatchback down the bluff, toward the beach, when my mother asked Dan to pull to the side of the road. Dan and I loved Bolinas. Bolinas was rustic and beautiful—not manicured and beautiful like Wellesley, or rustic and flaky like the Berkeley flats of Dan's youth. Wild, inviting, and sublime, filled with driftwood and dogs, Bolinas captured so much about the life we wanted to lead. Our love of the town was not unique, at least not in northern California. Whenever the highway patrol posted a sign on Route One marking the Bolinas turnoff, a local tore it down.

Dan parked near the old Bolinas Bay Bakery. My mother fetched a small suitcase-sized box out of the trunk.

"Open it!" she said to Dan, her arms extending from a body that a cartoonist would have drawn as a pixie cut, bright lipstick, and tiny torso, balanced on a skyscraper of jeans. "We're so, so happy to have you in our family."

Inside the box Dan found a fancy leather satchel, hand-stitched and heavy, the equivalent of the string of pearls my parents had given my brother's Catholic (but raising their children Jewish) wife as an engagement gift. "Thank you, you guys—really. Thank you," Dan said, turning the leather over in his palms. The bag carried a lot of symbolic weight. The satchel was not a briefcase; it was a bag for carrying an important manuscript. My parents had noticed that Dan was a writer, and they supported our marriage anyway. "This gift really means the world to me. It really does," Dan said. He had tears in his eyes.

After hugs all around, my parents rebuckled themselves into the backseat of my car, and Dan steered us down Olema-Bolinas Road, toward the lagoon. At which point my parents asked the question I knew they were dying to ask, the question that might have prompted my mother's request to pull over the car, because now that Dan was welcomed into the family, she felt a right to ask: "What are you planning to do about religion?"

We weren't planning to do much. Both of us had indulged manic fits of religious interest in our twenties. I'd binge-read the New Testament, Old Testament, Koran, and Siddhartha, and adored William James's *The Varieties of Religious Experience,* but I never felt anything sustained enough to call faith. Part of the problem was my still-unresolved annoyance with the Judaism of my childhood. I'd spent every Tuesday and Thursday afternoon at Hebrew school, in addition to Sunday school on Sundays, and, in my four years of three-times-a-week religious education, I learned only how to decode Hebrew letters into sounds—*ba-rook a-tah*—but not what the Hebrew words meant. I found this infuriating, just as I found it infuriating to set spoons on the table with dinner each night, as per my mother's request, only to return the spoons unused, half an hour later, to the silverware drawer. I distrusted ritual for the sake of ritual. Nor did I like the fact that neither of my parents could read or understand Hebrew. The idea that *I* should spend my afternoons learning it (sort of) instead of them made me mad.

They'd both grown up in assimilated families, my father in Cleveland, my mother in Galesburg, Illinois. I didn't have a *bubbe* who made kugel or spoke Yiddish. I had one grandmother (my father's mother) who read T. S. Eliot and practiced yoga; another (my mother's mother) who volunteered at the museum, looked fabulous, and shopped. My grandfathers, too, spanned what a friend had once described as "the Book Jew/Money Jew spectrum." My father's father was the son of the faucet king of Cleveland. My mother's father was a hotelier and professional chef, best known for inventing the Reuben sandwich for a man named Reuben Kulakofsky who played a late-night poker game at the Blackstone Hotel.

My parents—really, my father—wanted to be more Jewish than their parents, and a major part of my father's plan was to make his children more Jewish than himself. This agenda was not popular with anyone in the family. My father's father, the faucet king, offered my sister fifty dollars *not* to get bat mitzvahed. (Why the hell would she want to embarrass herself like that?) I disliked the more-Jewish plan, too, but lacked the courage for true rebellion. So I kept attending religious school and shunted my defiance into resisting what Judith Shulevitz calls the "imperative to worship."

" 'Open my mouth so that I may utter your praise.' *Really?*" Shulevitz quotes the common Jewish prayer in her book *The Sabbath World*. "I was to ask God to move my lips so that I could utter words that would gratify his ego?" I felt the same way, in touch with the obligation of religion but not its depth. During my bat mitzvah, I tried to talk with my friends seated in the congregation from my perch up on the *bimah*. Even my father noticed I was just going through the motions and conceded that the evening "was not a shining moment." Still, afterward I was an adult in the eyes of the temple. So I quit.

Dan had followed a similar path. He stopped attending church at age nine or ten, as soon as Kit allowed him to spend Christmas and Easter mornings home alone. When we met, we'd both gravitated toward a vague spirituality, a belief in slowing down—sitting still on the beach at sunset, a reading in silence on the couch. Shulevitz called these things, beautifully, "temples in time rather than space." My parents were not impressed. They approached religion as they approached marriage: with devotion and practicality. They believed in institutions, in the concrete world. You joined a temple, a physical temple, and you donated to its capital campaign, because that was your duty: to support the community and to keep the Jewish numbers up. My father had once told me he'd had three children because he wanted to net a Jew. You take two Jewish parents, you produce three Jewish offspring. Community served. Still, the question of what Dan and I were going to "do" about religion—the concern about our interfaith marriage that the question implied—caught me by surprise.

"We aren't going to *do* anything," I told my parents.

My mother tried one more time, though I could see she already felt slightly undermined by her location in my car's backseat. "How are you going to raise ethical children?"

"Mom," I shot back, "don't even try to tell me religious people are more ethical."

Dan kept his mouth shut and his eyes on Olema-Bolinas Road.

In late May, about a week after the Kushner café debacle, I'd met my friend Emily, the psychiatrist who'd referred me to Holly and others, for dinner at a restaurant called Flour + Water. She and I have the kind of friendship I should have had with Monique—an individual friendship, not one contained within or filtered through my marriage. As always, Emily was eager to hear how the interventions were going. Over pasta and a few glasses of wine I told her about Rabbi "Shit Storm" Kushner.

"You know what you need to do?" she said, laughing, toward the end of our meal. "When your girls are older, you need to get them interested in Jewish men. Then they get married and have Jewish families, and everyone will be happy."

I set down my spoon and paid the check. I thought this was brilliant (especially given that I was not interested in becoming more devout myself). Or at least I thought it was brilliant until I drove back home, up and over the grassy knob of Bernal Hill, and found Dan downstairs, half asleep, pillow over his head.

"I figured it out!" I whispered, pulling a corner off his ear.

"What?" Dan grumbled.

"I figured it out. Or really Emily figured it out. The whole Christian-Jewish shit-storm thing. The girls will just marry Jewish guys. Then they'll end up being Jewish. It'll be great."

I'd been assuming at this point Dan would squint at me and say, "That's genius, honey."

He did not. "No," he said, ripping the pillow off his head and sitting up straight. "No fucking way. You are not going to tell my daughters they should absolutely never marry someone like their own father. Even though *you* did."

I saw his point a second later. What if he'd returned from a night out with his surf buddies and declared, "Guess what, darling? Figured it all out. We'll just make sure the girls date only Aryans. That's cool with you, right?" Even my father, when I told him the whole Kushner story, seemed to accept Dan's reasoning and the importance of keeping Hannah's and Audrey's religious identities blended. He respected Dan's desire to have his children linked to his heritage, too. My father also understood that defining the girls as *not* Christian would alienate Dan's parents.

But my father had a hard time holding on to these ideas. Soon he decided he needed his own marriage project—or rather, he decided he needed to make a project out of my marriage. He volunteered to organize a panel on interfaith families for the American Jewish Committee, an organization to which he'd belonged for fifty-four years. When he asked me if I would participate, I felt I couldn't say no. I didn't think to ask him why a seventy-two-year-old man who'd been married to a Jewish woman for forty-four years would feel the need to organize a panel on interfaith marriage, nor did I think to ask what he was hoping to accomplish. I didn't ask anything. I stopped thinking in that way that's so easy to do around one's parents. I said yes and then I forgot about the panel until a week before when, as instructed, I dialed into a conference call to rehearse the event.

This panel consisted of a rabbi (not Kushner), me, the writer Peggy Orenstein, and a family therapist. As we agreed would happen the night of the event, I told the story of my half-Jewish half-Christian marriage. Then Peggy told her story (the one the American Jewish Committee wanted to hear): She'd married a Japanese-American atheist but they were raising their daughter Jewish—candles on Friday nights, camp Ki-Tov in the summer. Then the family therapist declined to tell her story. She said that would be unprofessional.

The following day my phone rang: the family therapist, explaining that she'd decided she wanted to use her time on the upcoming panel to talk about *my* story, because, as she put it, not choosing a religion for our girls was "the harder way." Apparently I was still not thinking much because I told her this was fine. I even further explained my philosophy of raising interfaith children. Children deserve to know who they are. My daughters are half Jewish and half Christian. How can raising them as such be blameworthy or wrong?

The night of the live panel, I drove Dan's ancient Toyota truck over to the Jewish Community Center, eating my takeout sushi en route, careful not to drip soy sauce on my dress. A month or so earlier Dan and I had loaded a dozen old paint cans in the pickup bed but never taken them to the dump. Dan had also accumulated, inside the cab, a mountain of empty coconut water bottles, a few Muscle Milk containers, ten or so now-blackened banana peels, and a sea of coffee cups, detritus from his workouts and runs to Ports Seafood, where he bought from the fishmongers who stayed up all night for halibut, squid, and true cod. Hannah hated the truck. When Dan drove it to pick her up from school, her face would fall, embarrassed, and she'd say, "Really, Dad?" That night of the panel the mess inside the truck felt so un-Jewish that I couldn't face the ex-Mossad security guard who checked all vehicles before waving them into the JCC garage. I parked two blocks away, on the street.

As I entered the building's big, cold atrium—the product of a very successful capital campaign—I realized, for the first time, that I'd entered a trap. Of course, anyone who attended this event, at the JCC, would favor Peggy's story, not mine. I did not care quite enough about Judaism to make it a priority in my life, and that position felt bad to those who did. Still, I felt blindsided while sitting on the rickety stage when the family therapist began talking about me.

"I have to tell you, when I first heard Liz was going to publicly admit that she was doing both, I felt concerned. And I will also tell you that, yes, a friend even called to ask, 'Do you know Liz is doing both?' So what I wanted to talk about tonight is this: Why do we say, 'Liz, you're bad?' "

Excuse me? Why do we say *what?*

"If she said, 'My girls are not interested in swimming lessons,' we would not be having this visceral reaction. But this is about survival. This is about the Jewish people. This goes back to the fall of the Second Temple, maybe even further. Rabbi, correct me if I'm wrong." She took a moment to drop the Jewish trump card. "This afternoon, I spoke to another friend, a Holocaust survivor. . . ." Then she came around to her point: The way for the Jewish community to stop hating people like me was to start oozing so much niceness that I'd embrace my Jewishness. Following this, Dan, too, and his parents would see "that Judaism is fabulous and wonderful and warm and embracing," and decide to convert.

"Of course, we'd have to put a lot of energy into that," the therapist conceded. So in the event her friendliness offensive failed, she decided to wrap up her allotted eight minutes by pointing out a flaw in Dan's logic. Did he not realize our two daughters were girls, thus already unlike him? "If your husband wants a child like himself, maybe you should have a son."

I spared her the fact that we'd tried.

Following an awkward silence, the rabbi made an attempt to set the panel back on track. "I want to stress that we're all good Jews. Please go on, Liz. . . ." I told the assembled crowd that Dan was not interested in a new religion. He didn't want to become a Jew. But then I lost the stomach to keep defending myself. The minute the panel ended, I left.

Dan's crappy truck never looked so good. I loved it, just then—the old paint cans, the garbage. I felt desperate to be back home. Once there I kissed the sleeping girls and fell into Dan's arms and cried.

That pretty much ended the religion discussion in our house. Others, even within our extended family, may lament our choices. But Dan and I are in agreement. We agreed at the start of our relationship and, years later, we still agreed. This experience with religion threw one tenet of marriage improvement into stark relief. The snakes in the bushes of our marriage—the problems that exist between the two of us, the issues that arise from our characters and shared history—those seemed worth wrestling out. But we needed to protect ourselves against people's ideas of how our marriage was problematic. We needed not to invite into our home the snakes that lay in the grass.

11
Money

My parents told me as a child not to worry about money. "Just make enough that you don't have to think about it." This sounded like really great, even modest, advice until I grew up and found myself living in San Francisco, a town enthralled by pastured (not to be confused with "free range") eggs that cost up to nine dollars a dozen. You need a colossal amount of money not to worry about money in a town like that. And if you don't have a lot of money, you need to have a very good story explaining to yourself why you don't. I started working on my money narrative in my early twenties, when I first read Sara Davidson's essay "Real Property." She starts with the question: " 'Who is the rich man?' asks the Talmud." She then obsesses on love and real estate. Story of my life.

The question of who is rich, whose life had value, became mine, perversely, because Dan and I are not money people. We don't make that much. We don't spend that much. We don't like to think about money. We carry no non-mortgage debt. Yes, like everybody else, we'd like to be rich. We think we'd make very good and tasteful rich people. We even used to daydream a lot about what we'd do if we "got over," what kind of car we'd buy (our "good" car is our 1998 Subaru, with 113,000 miles on it), where our cabin would be. But richness doesn't seem to be our fate. We have good financial intentions, as evidenced by the existence of our Roth IRAs and SEP IRAs and 529 college funds. But we don't deposit as much as we should. Our actions tend to fall flat.

This unimpressive fact is less impressive still in the context of my family. Nobody besides me bothers asking questions like "Who is the rich man?" They don't need to: They know. They all have MBAs. Whatever epigenetic accident failed to trip my financial switch happened early. You know those iconic photographs we all have of our childhoods, the ones we look at as adults and realize that our true natures were written all over our bodies long before we thought those natures had formed? In one iconic photo of me, taken by my mother when I was six, I'm riding a bike with my feet on the handlebars. In one of my brother, when he's about the same age, he's sitting behind a desk, holding a green crayon, ready to sign a deal.

Shortly after Hannah's birth Dan and I decided we ought to take advantage of my family's collective financial wisdom. We happened to be in Omaha for Thanksgiving, at my aunt Mary's house. Dan was looking huge, Western, and extremely uncomfortable, his hand glued to his mouth, covering the gap between his teeth. In our first forty-eight hours there we'd exhausted the short list of things to do (movie, Bikram yoga class at my second-cousin Tippy's studio). So with tiny Hannah asleep on my shoulder, we approached my father, who happened to be eating Corn Flakes, and asked what he thought we needed to do to be financially responsible, now that we were parents and all. My father enjoyed questions like this. He could be hard to talk to, but he wanted to help.

"You should probably have $100,000 cash or however much you

need to live on for a year, whichever is more," he said, setting down his spoon as he looked up from the *Omaha World-Herald.*

That pretty much ruled out being responsible.

But eventually we stabilized. By Audrey's birth, out of sheer panic, Dan had finished his novel—*whole life creative act, whole life creative act*—and started making decent money as a journalist. We didn't earn enough money to get over, or even get ahead, but we weren't falling behind either. The major weakness in our finances—besides the petrifying specter of our broke old age—was our willful blindness to them. Dan could not look at a bank statement without wanting to braise some pork. I could glance at our balances, but only through my fingers, as if watching a horror movie. Both now over forty years old, with two kids, neither of us tracked how much we spent, nor even how much we made until each April when I tallied our receipts and 1099s. We relied on what we called "emotional accounting." We vibed our balances, on our separate accounts no less. This worked well, almost too well, like guessing the time without a clock. When either Dan or I wanted to make the other squirm, we'd quote a line we'd overheard at a party. One of Dan's college friends, arriving straight from work, asked his wife what she'd done that day.

"What do you *think* I did today, sweetie?" she said. "I took money out of the ATM and lit it on fire."

So in an effort to buck up, some might say grow up, during the summer of our marriage improvement I decided to rationalize our money scene. We hadn't been fighting about money, which you'd think after the religion debacle would have given me pause. But live and learn—at least eventually. Besides, as I read in *Financially Ever After* by *Wall Street Journal* writer Jeff Opdyke, "The person sharing your bed will not be the person who causes the friction in your relationship; it's the person sharing your bank accounts and credit cards who will."

I decided we needed to make two immediate reforms: one, quit vibing our balances; and two, create transparency, otherwise, according to

Opdyke, our spending habits could become secrets and, soon thereafter, problems.

When I agreed to marry Dan, I agreed to marry California. Dan was broke, and California wildly expensive, but the joint commitment didn't seem like such a bad deal until we tried to buy a house. At that point, mid-1999, everybody who wasn't foolishly inhibited by some dumb idea like "I'm not a money person" was chasing the dot-com bubble. Houses sold for cash—in bidding wars, at open houses. You could get a job, as Dan's sister Kelly did, curating an online photo gallery that nobody looked at, and they'd pay you six figures plus pick you up in a chauffeured van and dry clean your laundry while you worked. But I was the kid with my feet on the bike handlebars, and Dan was worse. We still had a small pile in the bank, from my rocket book advance, and judging by the real estate listings, this was enough for us to buy a modest place in Bernal Heights. We weren't yet married, but that didn't bother me. I didn't want our savings to fritter away. So we called up a real estate broker and arranged to meet at the Martha & Brothers Coffee Shop, half a block from where we now live. Alongside the highway patrol cops playing dominoes, I told this broker our budget and showed her some listings that appealed to us, including one really adorable farmhouse on Jarboe Street. She glanced, nodded, and shoved the listings back toward me. "Almost everything is selling for twenty percent over asking," she said.

"What do you mean?"

"I mean just that. Everything is selling for way over asking. You should expect to pay about twenty percent more than the list price." Translation: Our math was wrong. This booted us down from an adorable farmhouse to a one-bedroom condo—not auspicious given that we both worked from home and we wanted to have kids.

But from my mom I'd learned to tap into a soldierlike energy, even an optimism, especially under stress. I said, "Well, we want to buy sooner rather than later, so we need to find something that works for us."

The agent liked my desperation. "Okay!" she said, standing and shaking my hand. "Let's do this."

I might as well have stenciled SUCKER on my forehead.

Making matters worse, a whole lot worse, the following week I had foot surgery. I won't bore you with the details. I don't think the human mind is capable of interesting writing about recreational running. (Calculus, the Sistine Chapel, yes. My ten-miler at 8:43 pace, no.) I'll leave it at this: I ran. I ran a lot. I hurt my feet. A doctor broke and reorganized some bones—in both feet, at the same time. Post-op, once the anesthetic block in my legs wore off, I took Percocet, and the narcotic haze paired up poorly with our real estate quest—which by that point our agent had convinced us was not just futile but also urgent. Housing prices were climbing by the week! Time was money, a lot of money. So after five loopy days scooting around my apartment on my ass, I lowered myself down the stairs, one riser at a time, to our agent's black Mercedes. She had a house to show us. The Prentiss Street House.

The Prentiss Street House was a 24-foot-by-32-foot-by-10-foot box with no foundation, no basement, no garage, just a chihuahua-sized yard, on far-from-gentrified Prentiss Street. Running down the middle of the house was a bearing wall. On one side of the wall the builder had crammed an open living room, dining room, and kitchen; on the other side, two bedrooms and a bath. The house had no place to expand and no charm. We later met a family who owned a replica of this house, on a different block. The husband had dug out a basement, by hand, with a shovel, because he needed a music studio and a place to lift weights. The digging took two years. After he finished, he and his wife divorced.

For reasons I can no longer explain, beyond the Percocet, we bid. We bid high. We bid 20 percent over asking—every dollar we had, just as our Mercedes-driving agent suggested. Dan was not on drugs, but this was not *his* money. (He didn't have any.) Besides, he'd grown up in

California and watched his father's secretary, along with countless family friends, amass huge fortunes, one unimpressive real estate deal at a time. But Kit and Dick did not do this. In a fit of Zen nonattachment, they'd decided against buying a $10,000 house at Stinson Beach because that seemed like a lot of money in the late 1970s. Now that house was worth $2,000,000. Dan mentioned the house about once a week.

The afternoon after we bid on Prentiss Jennifer called, ecstatic: "You got the house!" Something about those four words started burning off my Percocet fog. That evening Dan and I drove to Corte Madera, where he was reading at a bookstore, and by the time we crossed the Golden Gate Bridge I knew we couldn't sign. Our agent huffed, made empty threats, but agreed to meet us in the morning with a key. That night I skipped my Percocet. No more Prentiss Street House.

For months, as I convalesced on Advil, we lowballed a bunch of properties. Our agent temporarily quit. Then Dan noticed an especially dumpy-looking house on Ellsworth Street, covered with asbestos tiles and occupied by tenants, which in boom-time San Francisco were nearly impossible to dislodge. In theory this house on Ellsworth had "good bones"—at least in the sense that nothing was rotting. But really, the house was janky and under-framed, slapped together right after the 1906 earthquake as a bunkhouse. All the rooms opened onto a central hallway, each as characterless as the next and exactly the same size. Still, Dan argued, this was a great, maybe even the only, house for us: 750 square feet in the upper flat (where we would live), the same in a rental unit below, along with an unfinished basement, an attic, and an overgrown yard. I didn't see the allure. The downstairs carpet reeked of cigarettes and cat urine. The upstairs walls had been painted blood red. Yet on Dan's urging, we bid—and won, though none of our friends would have called it that. Dan drove by the house with his surf buddy Matt. Matt said, "Oh." The tenants stopped paying rent and refused to leave. We found a bed of nails and a shrine to rent control, when, six months and $7,000 in lawyer's fees later, we managed to move in.

By that point we were nearly busted financially. We made a stab at cheering the place up on the cheap with new IKEA cabinets and a vintage claw-foot tub. I even felt proud and optimistic, for a while. Then, in what would become a recurring pattern, my enthusiasm would fade. I'd repaint a room, refinish a dresser, buy a new striped cotton rug.

"Doesn't it feel like a beach cottage?" I'd say to Dan. The delight would last a week. Then I'd slide back into seeing our house as a drafty, chopped-up warren of rooms, hopelessly too small.

Easing the space pressure, shortly after Hannah's birth, the downstairs tenant suggested that he could move out, for a small price. This was extortion, plain and simple—we later learned he'd bought a house with his girlfriend—but we needed the room, so we threw him the very last of our savings, took over the front half of the lower unit for our offices, and rented out the back to Dan's sister Kelly, who'd just broken up with a boyfriend in Seattle and wanted to move home. Now, to reach our desks, we "commuted" out the front door and down the front steps, reentering the building at street level. This felt great, too, for a time. But then we both became annoyed that our living quarters were so tiny while our offices were relatively big. To discharge our frustration, we haggled over wall art. Dan believed that, along with the bad textile gene, I'd inherited a taste for soulless interior decoration, the kind you'd find in hotels.

"I mean, look at this stuff," he said, pointing to a cluster of four small framed black-and-white photographs I'd hung in our dining nook. "What is it with your family? Why the insistence on being generic? You learn absolutely nothing about the people who live here by looking at this."

"Those are my grandparents," I said. "My dad's parents, my mom's parents. The one in the lower left is my grandfather with Carl Sandburg."

Dan laughed, tried to apologize. The next week he retrieved from our basement a poster-sized photo of his father rock climbing El Capitan, in Yosemite, and nailed it above our couch.

A couple of years later Audrey arrived, a bomb of crazy energy who liked to nurse every ninety minutes, prompting Hannah, at age three, to describe nights at Chez Weil Duane as "I woke she and she woke we." This "we," of course, included me, but not Dan, who lacked the breasts that served as Audrey's late-night snack bar. He started slipping out the front door every night at bedtime to sleep in the spare bed behind my writing desk. The office, unfortunately, had no bathroom, so he'd bring along a Mason jar as a chamber pot. I consented to this sleeping arrangement—two exhausted parents seemed worse than one. Still, I hated the nightly click as Dan walked out the front door. Then came the morning that Dan left his Mason jar on my desk. That was the day I began viewing our housing situation as half-empty.

We'd already established that we couldn't move. I lobbied hard (and in hindsight, idiotically) to refinance with one of those five-year-fixed, interest-only loans that brought down the economy so we could finance a gut remodel. But Dan—proving the exception to the rule "there's nothing to fear except fear itself"; fear of debt is great—said no, absolutely not. More infuriating, he bolstered his arguments with half-assed hippy-isms. He'd learned just enough Eastern philosophy as a kid, running around the Green Gulch Monastery, to be righteous and indignant. "You know desire is the root of all suffering, right?" he'd say to me. "It's never going to end. We'll fix up our house, you'll be happy for five minutes, then you'll want an even nicer house."

"Wait a minute, baby. You don't know that. That's not true. I just want to live in our house in a better way."

"Oh, c'mon, that's crap. You don't want to live in this house in a better way. You want to live in a nice big antiseptic house, like the house you grew up in."

"No, I don't," our argument looped. "I want to live in this house, with you. . . ."

Among the deeper reasons I found this infuriating: I did not want to be seen as a materialistic dolt. I wanted to be viewed as beautiful and sparkling (though in my confusing way I didn't want to hear too much about it). Many of marriage's dark pundits describe the institution as being primarily about containment and control. They argue that all those who are happily married have Stockholm syndrome, they're in love with their keepers, clinging to their spouses despite what Laura Kipnis describes as "routine interrogations," "surveillance," and "impromptu search and seizure." "Like seasoned FBI agents," Kipnis writes in *Against Love*, "longtime partners learn to play both sides of the good cop/bad cop routine, '*Just tell me, I promise I'll understand. . . . You did WHAT?!*' "

I hated the idea that Dan was the velvet-gloved enforcement arm of the police state. I didn't want to see us as domesticating and babysitting each other, as patrolling against each other's least civilized impulses. And I didn't want to think that if we failed—if the lion didn't behave like a house kitten—we'd put ourselves under the receivership of a therapist, to have our vows enforced. Yes, Dan and I had kept each other on short leashes at times, checking in constantly via cell phone, following Kipnis's script (*Just tell me . . . You did WHAT?!*). But I didn't want a marriage based on compliance, a marriage dependent on rooting out desire. I preferred, with unusual romanticism, a marriage based on Stendhal's crystallization theory.

As Stendhal explains in *On Love,* "In the salt mines of Salzburg, they throw a leafless wintry bough into one of the abandoned workings. Two or three months later they haul it out covered with a shining deposit of crystals." This is what we do for our lovers: We endow them with "a thousand perfections." We see them "as something fallen from Heaven." Illusory and scary, yes, but I found Stendhal's far preferable to Kipnis's view. After meeting Dan, Joe Cocker's anthem "You Are So Beautiful to Me" always made me cry. Especially the words "to me." The beauty Dan saw in me came from him. *He* saw me as beautiful. What if he stopped?

Finally, Dan sensed the folly of insisting on viewing me and my relationship to our house at their worst. So, he proposed a compromise: installing an interior staircase to connect our offices with the rest of our home. We agreed he should not build these stairs himself. He'd been so miserable building the ones in the front of our house (hating doing something extremely important for which he felt not at all qualified—which also happened to describe the predicament of being a new father). Yet as soon as we agreed on this modest plan, we hit an impasse: Nobody would take the job. Building the staircase required first removing a defunct chimney Sheetrocked inside a wall. This made the task too big for a handyman but too small for a contractor. For a time we thought we'd cracked the problem: We found a former architect eager to work with his hands again. He proposed building a fabulous-sounding Japanese staircase, economic and with a small footprint. We agreed on a price, a tentative start date. Then never heard from him again.

"Do you think the world is trying to tell us that you were right?" I offered Dan. "That we should just accept living in our goofy home?"

Dan smiled, showing the gap between his teeth. The next day I returned from the playground with the girls to find a huge hole in our hallway floor. I peered down, to my office. Dan there stood with his Sawzall, framing the opening to the stairs.

That hole led to the removal of the defunct chimney and the demolition of several walls. Which led in turn to the revelation that our house felt drafty because our walls were made of paper and shims. Also this sad fact: Part of our foundation really was crumbling, though not where Dan had been drilling in the tie-down bolts a few springs earlier. The decrepit part was in the front. This should have been horrible, and in terms of the frantic magazine-article writing required to pay for the materials to shore up our walls and cap our foundation, it was. But Dan and I had found a sweet spot between us, a shared, if implicit, set of values for making decisions about our home and how to live in it. The cornerstone was, in effect, to marry the house: to stop talking about moving, to assume we'd raise our family here, to shape the space into what we needed. Or at least to shape it as much as possible without taking on debt.

Our life became a hologram: small shift, new angle, striking change. Now, upending the house felt exhilarating. We owned the place, right? It belonged to us. We could make it our own. Well, Dan could. He was the one holding the pneumatic nail gun. Enthralled by his tools—his manhood, his power, even his ability to make his wife supremely happy while making a huge mess—Dan's vision expanded. He caught what we called "mission creep," deciding that if he was going to build a staircase into our old offices, thus turning those offices into a construction zone, he really should first build a new office in the unfinished basement, so we'd have a place to work, a locale for earning money as the project unfolded. Concurrently, to speed progress, Dan hired a day laborer, an eighteen-year-old named Antonio who worked incredibly hard for his fifteen-dollars-an-hour plus lunch and then one day didn't show up. Dan drove up and over Bernal Hill, to the corner of 26th and Folsom Streets, where the *jornaleros* hang out each morning waiting to be offered work. There Dan found Antonio slumped on the sidewalk, head between his knees. In broken English Antonio explained that his seventeen-year-old wife had died, back home in Chiapas. Dan put Antonio in his truck, fed him breakfast, bought him the new sneakers Antonio improbably requested, then drove him to the airport. The next day Antonio's brother, Florentino, appeared at our house. The day after that Florentino arrived with yet another brother, Nicolas.

Dan loved the brothers. He even loved them on the day Florentino and Nicolas knocked on our door at 7:00 a.m. to see if they could please get paid for the week right then (it was Thursday and normally they preferred to be paid once a week, on Fridays, to minimize the mugging risk) as their fourth brother, Carlos, had just crossed the border with a coyote and was currently just across Ellsworth Street, locked in a windowless van. Dan ran down Cortland Street to an ATM. The next day Carlos, gaunt and leathery, came to work, too.

"Um, honey?" Dan would call my cell on weekends, when I tried to keep the girls out of the noisy, dusty house. "I decided to go a little bigger. I demo-ed the hallway." "I decided to move the bathroom." "Are you sitting down? I just told the guys to pull out all that old blown-in insulation in the attic so we can finish it and put a loft office up there."

This took prodigious amounts of money, lit on fire in the form of paying "the guys." It also turned our home into what Dan's best man, Russ, a State Department lawyer, described as "a toddler death zone"—holes in the subfloors from dropped tools, wiring in open walls.

We approached our home improvement the only way we knew, as writers. We viewed rough construction as rough draft. I had two jobs. My first was editor. How did the space feel? Good? Proceed. Bad? Rip it up and try again. My second job was project manager. I procured hard goods—windows, flooring, tools—and tracked the ebb and flow of our bank accounts. Thus it was my duty, shortly before Dan's fortieth birthday, to report that, irrespective of my supposedly bottomless desire to spruce up our nest, we needed to stop hemorrhaging money and quit. In the preceding nine months Dan had built an interior staircase; insulated all the walls; transformed the unfinished spaces in the basement and attic into home offices; installed hardwood over our busted-up Douglas fir subfloors; opened up the kitchen and dining room; moved the bath from the second floor down to the first; framed out a walk-in closet; and plumbed and installed a half-bath upstairs. The day I delivered my cease-and-desist order we ripped the filthy construction paper off the floor and Dan stashed his tool belt for good. On that day, as now, our master bathroom had no door and the pendant light above our dining room table hung by a knot. In fact, our house remains in this exact state, a DIY Pompeii. I would recommend our process to no one. It was perfect for us.

Now, three years later, spring-cleaning my marriage, I decided I ought to follow Opdyke's advice and create financial transparency, which I did by wrestling all of our account numbers onto one of those websites that renders every dollar you earn, spend, save, or borrow into colorful, nonthreatening pie charts. It didn't look so good—nor did it look so bad, either. Our house had appreciated a lot, meaning we had some net worth. And when you tallied up the sums from all our small savings accounts—the little SEP IRAs and Roth IRAs and 529s—we appeared to be people who cared, at least moderately, about our futures. Maybe, when the girls were ready for college, we could finance their educations at the University of California by borrowing a third, drawing a third out of our savings, and paying a third from our incomes. Still I worried at times about our economic codependence. For instance, Dan would get a parking ticket and I wouldn't pay it, on the theory that Dan needed to feel the pain and remember to feed the meter. But then Dan wouldn't pay the ticket either and we'd incur a late fee, at which point—worst of both worlds—I'd pay the ticket plus penalty so the fee didn't rise higher.

One night I loaded the new financial software app onto Dan's iPhone. I pulled up the graphs of our finances on his screen just before bed. As I'd read in Opdyke, each partner in a marriage needs to "open his kimono" and, more saliently, at least in my household, each partner needs to look. I promised Dan the visuals would not be scary.

Dan picked up his phone, squinted. A week later the app was gone.

I retreated to Opdyke once again. But after his suggestion of "the gift of a few hours with a fee-only planner" for a financially disinterested mate, I realized this was not going to work. My parents offered us each year "the gift" of a meeting with *their* financial planner. This happened in the lobby of an airport Hilton. Dan never came.

Then fate intervened in the form of an editor from *Bon Appetit*: How would I feel about an experiment—feeding our foodie family of four on $200 a week, the amount calculated to be a "modest" food budget by the USDA?

This became its own marriage experiment. "This is kind of your fantasy, right?" Dan said as we walked into Trader Joe's. We had not grocery shopped together, as equals, in six years. The effect was not romantic now.

I picked up a package of Niman Ranch center-cut pork chops, $5.49 a pound.

"What about fish?" Dan said. "Should we save money for fish?"

"I'd rather have that anchovy pasta one night and buy a six-pack of beer."

Dan shook his head and said, "Oh my god," as if I'd suggested Wonder Bread and heroin.

From my software program I knew that we spent a shocking amount of money on food—more than we did on our mortgage. But by that point we were all really getting something for it. Dan had eased up on the obsession (no longer bringing his sourdough sponge with us in the car, so that he could feed it if we drove to Berkeley for the day). His father had fallen in a rock climbing accident, breaking a vertebra. Cooking his dad a steak on his first night home from the hospital, Dan became interested in food as love—food as sustenance, generosity, and balm. He started perfecting chicken fingers and french fries for the girls; braises and fish stews for me. I now felt proud when friends happened over for dinner. Sweetly, Dan used a dishtowel to wipe stray sauce off the rim of each plate. He garnished Hannah's and Audrey's pasta with parsley, wanting to give them beauty, too. But food was still really his domain. Our kitchen was *his* kitchen. He labeled each shelf and the lip of each drawer with a Sharpie marker on painters' tape—SPATULAS & WHISKS, STRAINERS & SIEVES—so that I would adhere to his storage system.

Food purchasing, too, was in Dan's fiefdom. I liked the food budget. It made me feel controlled and virtuous. Besides, $200 is plenty of money, even in San Francisco, especially if you have the time or inclination to make beans and farro, or salt-cod croquettes, or if you whip up (or have whipped up for you) some buttermilk biscuits to go with the chicken soup you've made from the carcass left over from your two chicken meals (braised legs and stuffed breasts).

Sticking with the budget also put us back in touch with the simple pleasures of giving and receiving. I felt extra grateful to the neighbors and family members who are continually feeding my children. I also felt happier than usual to feed Cuya and the other kids who jumped on the trampoline and then knocked on our back door for food. Plus the regular-ness of our dinners—the chicken soup and biscuits—was a huge psychological boon. Since my teens I'd been studying the "regular" habits of gentile boys. I craved toasted ham and cheese for dinner. Meanwhile Dan had "regular" perfected by age fourteen. (No bratwurst sandwiches for him.) He wanted his life to be exceptional, a desire he expressed by making warm skate salad on a hectic Wednesday night. To Dan the budget was neither special nor pleasing. It was like any other kind of diet: confining, boring, a thing to endure. So much so that by day three he'd grown yet more fixated than ever with weightlifting, storing a long dowel behind the couch to practice his split jerk, which he'd come to believe he was doing wrong. He started upping the ante. No more plain-Jane chicken for us. On our fourth night he made a caramelized onion frittata. On our fifth, an octopus daube. On the sixth night, arriving home later than usual from the gym, Dan ratcheted up his game again.

"My big mistake was looking at Keller. Always a big mistake," Dan said, a FEMA-worthy mess in his wake, when he finally brought to the table the pork loins, which we had bought in the end, accompanied by asparagus mimosa and an electric green asparagus coulis. The kids' dinner had gone sideways, too. While Dan was preoccupied with the coulis, Hannah had installed a layer of nonregulation spicy pepperoni under the cheese on the entire pizza, and as a result Audrey, who'd had a horrible day at preschool, wouldn't eat a second bite. I was irate. One of the biggest luxuries, I realized, of not being on a strict budget is that the pizza can be rendered inedibly spicy, at least to a four-year-old, and you just make something else. Yet, once again, by bedtime, peace had been restored. Audrey had consumed a big piece of bread slathered in butter. I read *The Sabbath Box* (the girls still adored the offerings from their Jewish book subscription). Then I finished loading the dishwasher and walked downstairs.

"Marriage is a lot of *work,* don't you think?" Dan said the following and final afternoon, packing his bag for the gym. He was joking but also warning. We tried to avoid the *w* word—*work.* Its deployment did not go over well now. Neither Dan nor I wanted our union to feel laborious. We had not sought in each other economic stability. Had such economic stability been our goal, we'd both have been better off with different people, and everybody knew it. We'd married each other—and our marriage was good—because we shared a vision of a life. We wanted to focus on and embrace the present, with modest concessions to the future. We strove not to overvalue money. We believed (perhaps deludedly) that if we needed cash at some point we would be motivated and able to make it. So we abandoned our run at conventional financial advice, a decision we both understand will lead to some regret-filled days ahead.

For dinner, on that last night of our $200-a-week food budget, Dan grilled and thin-sliced an ox heart; he'd heard the creatine in it was good for muscle recovery. Then he handed me our remaining five dollars, enough to take the girls out for ice cream. My primary feeling at ending this experiment was relief. The $200 limit itself was not a big deal, but the focus on money was stressful. The happiness I shared with Dan, the life we built together, was not extravagant or materialistic, but it was particular and it was ours. I did not want to jam our good marriage into someone else's vision. I did not want to take our fine, idiosyncratic life and leave us muttering, like Laura Kipnis, "Work, work, work . . . When did the rhetoric of the factory become the default language of love . . . ?"

12
Monogamy

Monogamy is the most basic concept of modern marriage. It is also its most confounding. In psychoanalytic thought, the template for monogamy is forged in infancy, a baby with its mother. Marriage is considered a mainline back to this relationship, its direct heir. But there is a crucial problem: As infants we are monogamous with our mothers, but our mothers are not monogamous with us. That first monogamy—that template—is much less pure than we like to allow.

"When we think about monogamy, we think about it as though we are still children and not adults as well," notes psychoanalyst Adam Phillips. This was certainly true for us. On our wedding day, Dan and I performed that timeless ritual: I walked down the aisle with my father. I left him to join my husband. We all shed what we told ourselves were tears of joy. Dan and I promised to forsake all others, and sexually we had. But we had not shed all attachments, naturally, and as we waded deeper into our marriage and how we might improve it, the question of allegiances became more pressing. In our continuing sessions with Holly we'd tried not to stir the pot of our relationship too egregiously, yet the question still kept bubbling to the surface: What did our commitment mean? Was the monogamy in our marriage from the child's perspective (you belong to me alone) or the mother's (I belong to you, and I also belong to others)? Was our monogamy pure and absolute or was it interwoven with threads of fantasy? Did my love for Dan—must my love for Dan—always come first?

This all reached a crisis, predictably, during a summer weekend in Napa, in the worst fight of our marriage. More than food, or money, or my hapless notions about religion, we still fought about our weekends there. I'm not a golf lover or a fan of gated communities, but I liked staying with my folks at Silverado: out of the fog, free grandparental day care, a quiet road on which the girls could learn to ride their bikes, warm evenings to putter around barefoot, no-pressure meals with three generations, cousins with whom to play gin rummy, days on which the kids changed from pajamas into swimsuits and back into pajamas again. Dan hated it, every leaf blower, every golf cart. And his discomfort hadn't waned. Not only was Silverado anathema to his Berkeley upbringing, it reprised a long-standing fight between Dan's parents, from his childhood. Dan's maternal grandparents, the Howards, had lived in tidy, conservative Hillsborough, a suburb not unlike Wellesley, on the peninsula now known as Silicon Valley. During hot summer weekends, Kit often drove down with Dan and Kelly so they, too, could swim in her parents' pool. But Dick despised Hillsborough and usually refused to join. He loathed Henry Howard's patrician values—the Republican politics and penchant for clubs: two for golf (one on the peninsula, one in the city) plus the Pacific Union Club, on Nob Hill, where Caspar Weinberger sipped whiskey. Out of principle and need to protect a space of his own, Dick resisted almost all of the Howards' intrusions into his Yeats-reading, banjo-playing life. He even made Kit return the cashmere sweaters her mother sent her at Christmas. The world of cashmere was not the world of their marriage, the world she'd chosen in Berkeley, with him.

Up in Napa, Dan channeled his father. The sight of an ironed golf shirt made him furious. He drove an extra mile, around the outside of Silverado, to avoid entering through its front gate.

For the five years my parents had owned the condo, I'd tuned out Dan's complaints—they were childish, weren't they?—and scheduled Napa weekends whenever I wanted, assuming Dan would be happy to do as he pleased: come or, more likely, stay at home. I told myself this was not so bad. What new parent does not crave thirty-six or forty-eight hours solo? Certainly, I did. I'd been in a sticky, panicked rush since the minute Hannah was born, often leaving our car on our block much too far from the curb because I felt too frenzied to parallel park it well. Dan laughed at this, called my parking "self-expressive." But he didn't laugh about Napa, nor did I. Underneath Napa lay a tangle of subtext. Dan often wished he spent more time with his own parents, who treasured their peace and privacy. I felt an outsized obligation toward mine, as they'd moved from New England to be closer to us. We'd discussed this often, looping the same loop, since that first weekend at the Mill Valley marriage class. I knew that Napa made Dan feel angry and alienated—he'd told me a hundred times. He'd memorized my dutiful daughter routine: My parents were aging but healthy, our children loved being with them, and I knew that this couldn't last. The practical solution—the one to write on the calendar—was obvious to us both: Each month, in the summer, we should spend two weekends in Napa (down from the three I'd argued for), one weekend in "Dan's California" (the mountains or the beach, perhaps with Dan's parents), one weekend at home. But knowing the solution made no difference. We kept fighting because Napa rubbed a weak point in our marriage, a chink in our togetherness, our monogamy. How devoted were we to each other's needs? How much would we bend for the other? How fully did we keep each other in mind?

We'd approached this issue in other ways, among them: training to swim together from Alcatraz back to San Francisco. One piece of standard marriage advice is that couples should do novel activities together. Fresh adventures flood the brain with dopamine and norepinephrine, the same chemicals triggered by new love.

Dan did not immediately sign on for the swim. "You know this is two miles in freezing water, right?" he called up one night to the kitchen as I did the dishes and he minded the girls in the bath.

"Of course," I said.

A few days later, over a dinner of roast chicken and chard and caramelized onion gratin: "You realize there's a heavy current, and we'll get pummeled by chop, and it'll be really disorienting and chaotic in that way you hate."

"Yes, yes, I know."

A week after that, brushing our teeth: "This isn't going to be like floating around in the pool, like you did when you were pregnant. You're going to have to really train."

"C'mon, honey, I know I'll have to train. It'll be fun."

Dan relented and said yes.

Wanting my husband to think our ice-cold misadventure would at least be fun, I lined us up a swim lesson with David Durden, coach of the University of California at Berkeley men's swim team.

At the gorgeous Spieker pool, in Dan's hometown Berkeley sunshine, Durden asked us each to swim twenty-five yards. He then asked us to swim twenty-five yards back to him. Then he scratched his head. "Okay, let's start at the beginning," he said, as if he'd never seen anything quite like our strokes before. "Swimming is about efficiency. Think about feeling your body glide through water. Think of slipping, needling, not muscling through it."

Uh-oh. I stared at Dan through my goggles; he laughed at me. Despite his weightlifting, muscling through, we both knew, was my specialty. I'd been counting on a swim-training regimen pretty much exactly like my running one: an hour or so of heart-pounding, four or five days a week. Now I was supposed to calm down enough to slowly, painstakingly, needle through the water? Dan set one of his big hands on my head, jostled my swim cap a little bit. Maybe this *was* a bad idea.

In the weeks that followed, Dan hurled himself at technique, reading wonky swim-training manuals, watching YouTube videos of Michael Phelps, trying for that effortless grace. Meanwhile I couldn't resist approaching swimming as I approached everything else. After each pool session I'd text Dan my yardage—3,500! 4,000! 4,500! I'd always loved to earn a gold star.

A few weeks before our swim, we found a window to train together in the Bay, and the novelty of the open water caused the promised dopamine to kick in. Even just waiting for Dan by Aquatic Park, on the corner of Van Ness and Bay Streets, I felt, for the first time in years, like I was on a date—a *real* date, with someone who might unnerve or surprise me, not out on a date night, the pale married person's substitute. I'd been feeling extremely intimidated by Dan, by his diligence in apprenticing himself to a master, to his kung fu grasshopper's approach to learning. We changed into our wet suits at the Dolphin Club, an old-time mecca for open water swimmers, then met on the dock out back. Who was this man that I had married, his legs barrel thick from all his squats, his eyes, in contacts, out from under his glasses, once again electric blue? We stood for a moment on the small sand beach, then swam out toward the loop of buoys, and after we recovered from the sting of the cold water on our faces I immediately noticed a change: We'd switched from jousting with each other to battling the elements. Not man versus wife but couple versus the world. We formed a team, stroking side by side—no bickering, no ego, even gliding a bit. After swimming a mile I felt very cold but told myself not to panic, just feel the sensation and trust I'd be okay. Afterward, back in the Dolphin Club shower, my feet looked as purple as day-old bruises. But I didn't mention this to Dan, afterward on the sidewalk, as we walked arm in arm. I didn't want to ruin the moment.

The night before the swim Dan and I stood on the East Beach at

Crissy Field, looking at bright city lights reflected on the black water, the Marin County homes across the Bay glittering like jewels. Dan knew he was fit enough, and I was fit enough, but still his jaw clenched with nerves. He worried that Alcatraz Island looked so dark and distant, the water in between cold and deep. The weather forecast wasn't great, either, and Dan knew from all his years surfing that a small thing like wind could quickly transform the face of the ocean, turning a placid pool to a nausea-inducing roller coaster, each attempt to breathe resulting in a mouthful of sea foam. But I was optimistic, full of the romance of our impending adventure.

"I like you," I said to Dan as we stood on a low cement wall. He pulled me close as the moon rose over the headlands. Was *liking* the holy grail of the better marriage? We said "I love you" all the time. Like, in the midst of what Kazantzakis called the "full catastrophe," felt more special, unexpected, more conditional.

And then we jumped. After waking up at 5:45 a.m. and speeding across the water to Alcatraz in an open-topped inflatable Zodiac, we pulled off our warm hats and ski parkas, slid BodyGlide along our necks to prevent our wet suits from chafing, kissed Hannah, who'd come along for the ride, and jumped into the Bay. As with love, real love, vulnerability is everything. We leapt feetfirst, no gingerly half steps to take off the boat.

My first few strokes away from Alcatraz felt fantastic—strong and smooth. The air and water remained strangely still as the storm collected in the distance, and in my relief over the surface conditions I failed to notice the water temperature: It had dropped considerably since our Dolphin Club session, to a frigid fifty degrees. When I rolled to breathe, I could see Dan, his stroke graceful and loping, and there in that beautiful quiet of water, I felt so proud of him and so proud of us, exhilarated to be alone together in the middle of this huge watery expanse, in the middle of our big city, in the middle of our lives. We were not racing— we'd agreed not to from the start. We were just together, each moving forward, keeping track of our own bodies and each other's, occasionally craning to glimpse our Hannah's freckled face in the boat.

After twenty minutes I finally mustered the courage to look back, to see how far we'd swum. Except Alcatraz wasn't where I expected it to be. The current had pushed us much farther than expected toward the Golden Gate, and Angel Island was at my back. I lowered my head, tried to feel the cadence of my stroke. Then fifteen minutes later I stopped again and called out to Dan. I knew this was a mistake; I'd get too cold. But I wanted and needed to connect with him. My arms had started rotating clumsily. I'd swallowed some water. With each breath I'd started lifting the crown of my head, causing my body to sink. I no longer felt invincible as a solo unit. My mind felt dim and fuzzy. I was alarmingly hungry.

"Hey, baby, let's try to pick up the pace," Dan called out. But I wasn't in any position to move fast.

He just wanted me to warm up, I realized that later. But I couldn't think lucidly in the moment. All I could do was keep soldiering on, stroke after inefficient stroke. By that point, to prevent himself from streaming too far ahead, Dan had almost stopped swimming, each of his pulls many times more productive than mine. He'd freestyle one arm then the other, then lift his head again and wait. I could see the Palace of Fine Arts behind him, its gleaming, majestic dome a beloved remnant of the 1915 Pan-Pacific exposition for which all the other buildings had been torn down or moved. But then, finally, we could see our mothers on the beach, jumping up and down. Soon after, through the clear, cold water, my feet touched the sand below.

"Oh my god, we made it," I said, standing, reaching out for Dan's arm.

Our bodies were swollen, our faces had frozen into red masks, it would take me two days to warm up, but we'd done it. Normally you don't get to schedule a morning for a big change. You get sick or you fall in love, and transformation washes over you. Or else you decide to trek through India, and it takes a month. Or you try to find God, and it takes a lifetime. But here we were. We'd jumped into the Bay only seventy-five minutes earlier, and traveled only the distance of a nice, modest walk. Yet we'd slipped out of our daily lives and taken a dip in the unknown. Together.

Unfortunately, we lacked that same sense of joint adventure on the weekend of our awful Napa fight, in June of the summer prior. My folks were visiting friends on the East Coast. We'd just gone up with friends, Mike and Kiernan, but Dan hated Silverado more than ever. Friday night we ate dinner on the condo's deck, its eastern side shielded by a wall of Plexiglas, to fend off wayward golf balls. Over steak and red wine we discussed our friend Mike's father. Mike was an only child. His father, a divorcé in New York, was having an acute health crisis. Mike needed to be there, but how much? How was he to balance his father's needs, his duties as a son, with his duties to his wife, Kiernan? When he left she was alone with their one- and three-year-old children, her full-time job, their old wooden house, their rowdy dog.

The next morning, Saturday, I left to run before the sun rose too high. A couple of miles from Silverado I took a gamble, turning down a dirt road that turned out to be a dead end. I backtracked, returning a bit later than expected, and when I did, tired and dehydrated, I found Dan and the girls on an Astroturf putting green, Dan ranting about how he hated that all the houses looked the same, with tinted windows blocking the natural light, the golf course obliterating the landscape, all the assholes who played golf on it.

Good lord—why did Dan even care about the golfers? He never spoke to them. Couldn't he just let it go?

After I showered, Kiernan and I took the kids to the pool. The next day, Sunday, happened to be Father's Day, but that afternoon in town, shopping for dinner with what I thought were the best of intentions, I felt so infuriated by Dan's relentless crabbiness I failed to coax the girls into buying him a gift. The final insult came Father's Day afternoon, as we packed to go home. In the preceding weeks I'd thought Dan and I had made some progress. I'd agreed, for instance, for the remainder of the summer not to make any new plans involving Napa without consulting Dan first. But loading our canvas bags into our Subaru, I informed Dan that earlier I'd told my mother she could bring the girls up herself the following weekend. Dan erupted in rage.

"Those are my *actual* children. I, too, get to decide what happens in this family. Do I need to tell you to tell your mother, 'OK, Mom, I'm not allowed to make any plans for our children without getting permission from my husband?' Do I need to be telling you, 'I'm sorry, little girl, *I* make the plans in this family and *I'll* tell you what to tell your mother about where my children are going'?"

I stiffened and said, "Of course not."

"How far are you going to let this go?" Dan kept screaming. "Are you willing to get divorced so you can keep spending weekends with your mom?"

I stood up straight and froze in the still, hot air. I didn't want time to move either forward or backward. What if I said or did the wrong thing—made promises I couldn't keep or further tore open the rift with Dan? This was the first time in our marriage either of us had invoked divorce.

Like most married people, I imagine, we'd both thought about it idly. At least I had. When Dan was at his most depressed I'd close my eyes and picture an easier life *not together*, without his moods, raising the girls in tidy solitude. I'd devoured Ellen Tien's *O* magazine article "The Mid-Wife Crisis," in which she describes "the age of rage" that marks the middle of marriage, "the six-hundred-pound mosquito in the room" that is the possibility of divorce. (Tien writes, "I recently stood by as a designer, a mother in her 40s, announced to a group of women that she was divorcing her husband. The women's faces flickered with curiosity, support, recognition, and—could it be?—yearning.") I also tore into Sandra Tsing Loh's *Atlantic Monthly* bombshell, "Let's Call the Whole Thing Off," along with the accompanying video, shot in her newly rented ten-foot-by-ten-foot U-Haul storage unit. Loh, newly dispatched of her twenty-year ball-and-chain, faces the camera in her dusty kerchief, looking deranged, fabulous, heroic, like a domestic Che. She describes her "divorced person's oddly relaxed—oddly civilized, even horribly French?—joint custody schedule." She looks off balance and very alive.

Dan and I didn't discuss these articles (which I probably never could have compelled him to read, anyway) because we did not discuss divorce. No cheating, no dying plus a silent addendum: no divorce talk. I had a taboo against it, an almost primitive belief that the idea was so toxic one had to keep it in a hole, given no quarter, no light. The research was less definitive. In a paper titled "Does Divorce Make People Happy?" Linda Waite, at the University of Chicago, found two out of three unhappily married adults who avoided divorce or separation ended up happily married five years later. Yet in "Do Divorcing Couples Become Happier by Breaking Up?" Andrew Oswald, at the University of Warwick, found the opposite: Divorce, for both men and women who chose it, was a psychological boon. Now Dan had cracked the lid on our own divorce discussion, let the devil out of solitary, allowed it to play in the yard. Our drive home was horrible, earbuds jammed into the children's heads so they'd hear only *Mrs. Piggle-Wiggle,* not me calling their father an ass.

By the next morning, my anger had curdled into despair. I dropped the girls at school, then I sat with Dan on our front steps, feeling gutted and raw. Every house on Ellsworth Street had the curtains drawn in its front windows. This was crucial, for privacy, on such a narrow block, but now the endless panes of gauze felt obscurant and sad. Did all our neighbors, in all these houses, fight like this? Why were we fighting so badly now? We'd been working so hard, making so much progress. So how had we gone from being the most happily married people we knew to screaming about our own divorce? And how had we done so without an affair, a bankruptcy, an overt marriage-improvement disaster, or even a significant lie?

I cried again, watching the cars roll down the hill. A girl Audrey's age who lived across the street had almost been hit a year earlier by a crook fleeing a cop car. I felt the fragility of life, particularly of marriage. This was a bond based not on blood, only on emotion. In what sense was it a bond at all?

My head spun—disoriented, unhinged from the concrete world— as it had in the moments following Hannah's birth. After labor I'd held her tiny body for a moment before the pediatrician whisked her off to the NICU. Dan followed the Plexiglas bassinet, as did my parents. The delivery team cleaned up and left. I found myself alone, drenched in sweat, on a dirty hospital bed. Had I really just birthed a baby? If so, where was she now? That day, in that moment, I picked up the phone and called my aunt Connie, to keep myself grounded. I felt the same need now to reestablish footing, but Dan and I both felt scared to speak. Like in the moments after an accident, I didn't know how badly we'd been hurt. Eventually we bowed our heads and walked back inside, made coffee, tried to work. Had this all been a beautiful, horrifying dream?

The Thursday following our fight, as we entered Holly's office, I felt certain she'd side with me. Dan needed to get over his holier-than-thou Berkeley hang-ups. Sure, golf communities are snobbish and lame, but family was more important. Besides, I let Dan run amok in the kitchen and I dealt with the kids more than he did. So I got this.

Holly, in her lawn chair, did not agree. "It sounds like you've created these little enclaves of rationalizations. *I give on all these other fronts, so I'm entitled not to give on this one.*"

Right. I felt entitled.

"But that does pose a problem—for Dan. Because he feels he's really not taken into account."

For a few beats I did not quite realize I was losing this fight. I had not imagined how my devotion to my parents could put me in the wrong. But Dan brightened immediately. "Just as you were talking there, I was having all these fears come up again. I have a real fear of being an appendage in that family. A fear that Liz's real family is her and her mother and I was just a sperm donor. That it would be really fine if I disappeared. Nothing much would change."

"Really?" I asked. "You have that feeling generally?" I had thought through some of the ways I betrayed Dan with the girls. I often put their needs before his. Also, as they'd grown older, I'd noticed us forming cross-generational allegiances. Hannah and I would whisper about how we wished Dan wasn't so chronically messy and emotionally florid. Audrey would promise to take my place as Dan's perfect companion; she would do the things I wouldn't do: climb huge overhanging rocks, eat whole fried smelt. But still I was having a hard time letting myself see my culpability in the conflict with my parents. From certain angles I could glimpse it. I knew I made unilateral decisions and assumed Dan could fend for himself. Yet I felt so much closer and more dedicated to Dan than I did to my mother and father. We'd promised, that day on Guerrero Street, to "do everything together" and nearly followed through. Given our home offices, Dan and I often spent twenty-one hours in the same place. I adored my mother, but she and I were far less joined. I was not fully relaxed with her. I saved my unguarded self for Dan alone.

Again, at the end of our session, our conversation spilled out onto the sidewalk. I could not believe Dan thought my primary relationship was with my mother. "Do you feel that way in general, or just in terms of Napa?" I asked, pleading and mystified, hoping to define for myself a lesser offense.

Dan, so big and so handsome, and so angry, dodged the question, then declared it immaterial. "Will you just quit it with your rationalizations? Don't you get it? It doesn't matter when. You prioritize your mother over me, and that makes me feel like some fucking potted plant." Any rupture in our relationship, anytime, weakened the whole.

I accepted the any-rupture argument relative to sex. All physical infidelity was an infidelity to me. Still, I felt shaken and confused standing next to Dan's old pickup. I knew a better marriage meant a marriage that gave me more strength, more courage to face the unknown—that much was increasingly clear. Dan had faith in me, and that helped me have faith in myself. But what needed to change in our marriage for it to give more strength and courage to Dan, to make him not feel like a potted plant? Commitment is two-pronged, requiring dedication and constraint. Did I need to sacrifice more? Cut back parts of my life, as I had with Monique, to reap the symbolic power of renunciation and create a stricter fidelity? Did I need to make more room for Dan—constrain myself further—so that our marriage could encompass more of his hopes and feelings?

Back in Holly's office the following week we again discussed what I thought would happen if I let go of my rationalizations, if I let down some of the barriers I'd erected against Dan's needs. I tended to describe my relationship with my parents in terms of obligation, not desire. I'd tell myself that I *needed* to do all these things—go to Napa, show up at birthday dinners—for my parents, not for me. This framing, Holly coaxed me to see, shut down conversation and helped me skirt Dan. This was a family trait. Just a few weeks earlier, over lunch in Napa, my sister told me she *had* to spend the night there, leaving behind her husband back in Berkeley with their three young kids, because she *needed* to attend our aunt Connie's birthday brunch the following day. This construction—the obligation implied—was 98 percent malarkey. Yes, Connie was having a birthday brunch but my sister had then twin two-year-old boys and an infant daughter. Nobody expected her to wear clean clothes, let alone leave the house. Yet the obligation she fabricated was useful, even inspired. She *had* to go to the party. End of discussion. This produced ten hours of sleep, a morning swim at the spa, and a catered meal.

But Holly encouraged me to see the downside of such rhetoric—why it enraged Dan, left him feeling "emasculated," as she put it.

"That's definitely right," Dan said. "Remember when I blew up in Napa and said, 'What do I need to do? Do I need to tell you to tell your mother, 'OK, Mom, I am not permitted to make any plans regarding our children without discussing it with my husband and getting permission from my husband?' We don't live that way. We don't talk that way to each other, but I was generating that rhetoric because I didn't know what to do except to become that big asshole authoritarian husband."

Holly paused. "It sounds like we're seeing desperate effort after desperate effort to get through to Liz, because she expects you to be passive."

"It's not usually true," Dan said. "I don't normally think she expects me to be passive. But I feel like she's got this iron will on this issue. It's unlike any other issue in our lives."

"What do you think would happen if you let down that iron will?" Holly asked, turning to me. "What would happen if you let go of your rationalization?"

I had a hard time retaining the question. I felt it there in my mind, but then it slipped away. So Holly asked again. "What do you think would happen if you made yourself open to discussion, if you let go of the rationalization?"

Again I felt the query start to fade. The world of fair play felt so threatening. What if I fell short in defending my parents? What if I failed to be a good daughter? I worried I'd been too hard on them at times, my father in particular. If I let in Dan's arguments, I might be swayed to spend less time with my parents, and as a result I might disappoint them, and disappoint myself, leaving everybody (except Dan) sad and empty, the kids distant from their grandparents. I'd always lived a thousand miles from my own grandparents. I'd never known them well.

"I'd just be so vulnerable," I finally said to Holly. "I'd be like a beating heart with no rib cage."

"So, there's a feeling," Holly said, "that if you take Dan into account you're going to lose in a big way."

"Yes. I imagine I'm going to be squashed."

Holly sat up in her lawn chair. "We're going to have to stop for the day."

13
Sex

Since the beginning of this project, Dan had been waiting for one thing: our visit to the sex therapist. And I have good and bad news on this front: improving the sex part of our marriage was much easier than one might guess, and the process of doing so made both of us want to vomit.

This whole project had started because of sex, in a way. I don't mean to alarm you. I felt as defrauded as the next reader of *A Year by the Sea* when, after 151 pages of swimming with seals and walking on the beach with Erik Erikson's widow, the writer Joan Anderson comes around to saying, in one of the more thunderously forehead-slapping moments in women's literature, that perhaps the reason she felt the need to leave her husband of many decades and rediscover her womanhood in their Cape Cod cottage was that she hadn't gotten laid in "what seems [like] hundreds of years."

That was not our situation. Just the opposite. We had sex—regular sex, very *regular* sex. A few times a week, not terribly creative. I seemed to share a bedroom-*anschauung* with Nora Ephron's alter-ego in her novel *Heartburn*. "We hadn't been doing anything particularly inventive in that department of late, but I have never been big on invention in that department. Why kid around?" Still I thought Dan and I were doing well, commendably even, for a couple with such young kids. Then, late in the summer, while Dan was doing his pre-hab exercises, I read Stephen Mitchell's *Can Love Last? The Fate of Romance over Time* and had an honest-to-goodness revelation. In this brilliant psychoanalytic treatise Mitchell explains that romance doesn't die in marriage due to neglect. He argues that romance dies because we kill it, on purpose, as it becomes increasingly dangerous. Especially in marriages like mine, Mitchell writes, in which each spouse is a domestic one-man band—cradling an infant with the right hand, straightening a tie with the left, conference call pinned to the ear, kissing a spouse good-bye—we can't bear to think of our spouses as anything less than entirely predictable. We are too reliant on them.

Oh my. This is why the swim from Alcatraz had worked for us: It broke us out of predictability, pulled in more risk. Mitchell lays out the commonly held theories why romance degrades: "because time and success are its enemies"; "because it's driven by sexuality, and sexuality is very primitive in its nature"; "because it is inspired by idealization, and idealization is, by definition, illusory"; "because it easily turns into hatred"; "because nothing stays the same, especially people." Then in his cool, laserlike way, he tells us that he believes none of these theories, at least not entirely. None accounts for our complicity—our desire to mute romance's dynamism, our impulse to paint our spouses as knowable, our need to believe our mates can't play entrancing romantic leads. When a woman arrives at Mitchell's therapy office, bored by her husband (whom she claims to love) and under the thumb of a lover (whom she hardly knows), Mitchell doesn't ask the expected question: "Why do you find sexual excitement only with strange men?" Instead he asks, "Why do you think your husband is boring? How have you managed to convince yourself that he's utterly dependable and safe?"

The illusion that our spouse is some sort of golden retriever is "not a given but a construction," Mitchell writes. It's a chimera, a "collusive contrivance," a "protective degradation, a defense against the vulnerability of romantic love." We tell ourselves that our mates, who travel or go to work each day amid a sea of potential lovers, will return home, ever faithful to us, because we cannot bear to think otherwise. We weave stodgy muumuus for our husbands and wives on the looms of our anxieties. Then when our marriages implode, the outfits are shed and the truth is revealed. Says Mitchell, "The husband really was not so dependable; the wife was really not so devoted. 'She is not the person I thought she was,' is the lament of the betrayed. Precisely."

So who was Dan, under his Lucky Brand motorcycle T-shirt? I took him to be a serial obsessive, energetic, doting, manly, sensitive, a bit vain, with conventional tastes. But maybe I didn't really know. He'd been spending a lot of time at the gym lately, then coming home pickling radishes and red onions à la Thomas Keller's cookbook *Ad Hoc at Home*. Could this man really be straight? Thus inspired by Mitchell, I decided to try a thought exercise: to think, while Dan and I were making love, that I didn't really know him as well as I thought I did, that he was not predictable in the least. And somewhat shockingly, within a few minutes, for my husband of ten years—the husband with whom I'd tried to keep a de facto sex-every-other-night schedule—I started to have some of the same sweaty feelings I'd had in my twenties. I wanted to captivate, discover, beguile, be worthy. I wanted to let my psyche ooze and fuse as I had many years ago at the start of an affair.

This was great, right? This was the point. A better marriage meant more passionate sex, this went without saying. But in the preceding months I'd noticed a pattern: Improving my marriage in one area often caused problems in another. More passion meant less stability. More intimacy, less autonomy. This had happened from the beginning. After our first marriage education class we'd had some particularly ardent romps. But the mornings after I'd find myself pulling my hair into a ponytail, sliding on my glasses, eager to return to my own thoughts at my own desk, to cut off the dream. I did not quite know what to make of this. One well-established school of thought views sex as a metaphor for marriage. Its bards write rational-minded books like Pat Love and Jo Robinson's *Hot Monogamy,* in which they argue, "Good verbal communication is one of the keys to a good sex life. When couples share their thoughts and emotions freely throughout the day, they create between them a high degree of trust and emotional connection, which gives them the freedom to explore their sexuality more fully." But there's an opposing, and frankly more intellectually compelling, school that argues the opposite: that sex—even sex in marriage—requires barriers and uncertainty, and we are fools to imagine otherwise.

"Romantic love, at the start of this century, is a cause for embarrassment," moans Cristina Nehring in *A Vindication of Love: Reclaiming Romance for the Twenty-first Century.* Enough with the pathetically dull, supremely responsible companionate marriages like ours. We need "to rediscover the right to impose distances, the right to remain strangers." Nehring is aghast at those who strive for equality, particularly those who would strive for equality and still believe that they can think. According to Nehring, to be "inflamed intellectually," "we need to be enlisted emotionally." Without "emotional engagement, most people do not interrogate themselves about topics for which there is no immediate or pragmatic urgency"—that is, topics beyond what's for dinner or what kind of TV to buy. The editors over at *n + 1,* an intellectual magazine that describes itself as being "like *Partisan Review,* except not dead," share this sentiment: "If you commit to marriage," you win "the war for harmless cuddliness. To marry is the closest adult thing to making your eyes big, your forehead rounded, and your hands into adorable little paws. Look at hubby-wubby!"

Yet horrifying as all this sounded to me, I had to admit that my eros with Dan was on the careful side for a second, more worrisome reason: Our relationship had started on nasty footing.

"What's wrong?" I'd say to Dan when he'd look at me strangely during a post-lunch coffee break in Dolores Park, back in our earliest months together when we still kept separate apartments.

"Oh," he'd say, "I just don't like your glasses." Or, "I don't like your shoes." The worst of these Tourette's-like outbursts occurred on the phone. "I'm attracted to you sometimes," Dan said one afternoon. Right then I pulled on my black down parka—overkill for February in San Francisco, but it made me feel I knew who I was—and marched over to Dan's apartment on 20th Street.

"We're done," I said when he opened the oversized Victorian front door. "I can't be with someone who's attracted to me sometimes. I'm sorry. I love you. But being attracted to me sometimes is not enough. We're done." Dan stood motionless, alarmed but not surprised. "Really, I love you," I said, turning to walk back down the cement steps. "Call me if you ever stop being such a mess. I'll be the girl waiting by the phone."

Dan didn't say much. The conversation took two minutes. Walking home, I kept my eyes straight ahead, focused on the bodega where Dan bought Peppermint Patties. I was determined not to look back, not to let Dan see me cry. In that moment my pride felt important. The next day, as I knew he would, Dan called and asked me to dinner. To pick me up, he climbed the stairs to my apartment slowly, a supplicant in a sport coat bearing flowers. We ate moules marinière in South Park. In some sense we married then. A part of our love had always felt inevitable, and over our bowls of shellfish broth we pulled a belief in our togetherness into the center of our lives.

With that implicit commitment, Dan's rude outbursts ceased. He started working what Stendhal describes in *On Love* as the wonder of the salt mine, encrusting me with jewels. But he also continued writing his novel, the one that began as a memoir about the John Muir Trail but ended up about his ex-girlfriend. I tried to ignore this as Dan, then in his office next to mine, read *Candy* for inspiration and crafted love scenes so stirring one ended up reprinted in *Best American Erotica*. In those years, when friends asked me what Dan was working on, I'd say, "He's writing a novel about a torrid affair, and it's not about me." Fortunately, for our physical life, the novel was published to mixed reviews; by a few months post-publication it had disappeared. Still, I refused to compete with the book's antagonist with regard to eccentric sex. Perhaps for this reason Dan and I gravitated toward a stable point that well enough satisfied both of our desires and just stayed there.

Then, at my desk one glorious September day, I started reading *The Multi-Orgasmic Couple: Sexual Secrets Every Couple Should Know*. (Overachiever, at work on the sex unit.) I sent Dan an e-mail titled "Nine Taoist Thrusts."

From page 123 of *The Multi-Orgasmic Couple*:

From the seventh-century physician Li Tung-Hsuan Tzu:

1. Strike left and right as a brave general breaking through the enemy ranks;
2. Rise and suddenly plunge like a wild horse bucking through a mountain stream;
3. Push and pull out like a flock of seagulls playing on the waves;
4. Use deep and shallow teasing strokes, like a sparrow plucking pieces of rice;
5. Make shallow and then deeper thrusts in steady succession;
6. Push in slowly as a snake entering its hole;
7. Charge quickly like a frightened mouse running into its hole;
8. Hover and then strike like an eagle catching an elusive hare;
9. Rise up and then plunge down low like a great sailboat in a wild wind.

This e-mail was partly in response to one Dan had sent me a few weeks earlier, just to see how much he could tweak my type-A sensibility. It was titled "Strength Benchmarks for Women" and indicated I was supposed to be able to do ten pull-ups, twenty bar dips, front squat and bench press my body weight, and dead lift my body weight times 1.5. (I can do none of these things.) Upon receiving the thrust e-mail, Dan ran up from his office in the basement to mine in the attic and asked which thrust sounded best. This was a departure for us, as after my feeling rebuffed in some early attempts to make use of *The Joy of Sex* we'd received as a kitschy wedding present, we'd settled into our narrow bowling alley of a sexual life. I'd never quite shaken the sense that my role in Dan's life was to be the steady, vanilla lay.

High above noisy Franklin Street, in our sex therapist's office, Dan launched into an exhaustive sexual history. "When I was fifteen years old I was dating a girl. . . ."

I can't tell you how monumentally sick I felt hearing about Dan's ex-girlfriends. Could we *please* never discuss this again?

"We had this completely psychologically sadistic thing that was incredibly disturbing to me. Every few years I'd have a relationship that mirrored that one, and right before Liz I had the bull-moose loony of these relationships. From when I was twenty-nine to thirty, I had this one-year relationship that for me was totally off the deep end. It was like sticking my finger in the electrical socket of my own unconscious."

We'd come to see Betsy Kassoff, a so-called "self" therapist who had an outstanding reputation for dealing with sexual issues, not a psychologist who specialized in sexual dysfunction, because we weren't contending with that. Self-therapy is based on Jay Earley's idea that our psyches are composed of many parts, and that we all have competing sub-personalities inside us. Those warring factions (of which we are often unaware) cause us to hurt people we love. They undercut our goals. According to self therapists like Betsy, however, all parts of us, even the most seemingly irrational, deserved respect. This is a bighearted take on humanity. It made Betsy warm and approachable. She had eyes as blue as Dan's and a touch as deft as Bill Clinton at a barbecue. She sat in a chair that matched those set out for us. When Dan finished talking, she just said, "Wow."

We'd talked only around the edges of this before: the trauma of the bull-moose loony relationship, the unpleasant start. Not until five years into our ten-year marriage had either of us gained any clarity on this matter, and by that point we both felt desperate to pack it away. Strange, now, after months of spring cleaning our marriage, what relief we felt to be opening that rank old hamper. Betsy could not have said more than fifty words before Dan paused and I leapt in, explaining how he and I hadn't been talking to each other while having sex. And not making eye contact, either. "I guess I just look at you so much," I said, laughing at the absurdity of only now discussing this for the first time. "I want to be transported to another world."

"So you like the merger," Betsy said to Dan, summarizing. "And you have a little bit of a horror of it, Liz?"

Yes, correct.

"And what about the darker, more aggressive side of sexuality you talked about in your earlier relationships? Would you say it's been more difficult to bring those parts of yourself to this relationship?"

Betsy worked gently and efficiently, a nurse undressing a wound. I confessed my craving but also my worry that we could not be sexually aggressive without conjuring up Dan's bull-moose loony sex. Dan swore—eagerly—this was not the case. The layers of our erotic life kept pulling back. I allowed that I felt hemmed in by what I felt was my duty to be "regular," and annoyed that, in the context of our marriage, Dan supposedly had an important sexual history while I had none. We joked about that universal male fantasy—as Dan voiced it (playing the role of everyman speaking to every wife): "You were born a virgin, you met me, we had the greatest sex of your life, end of story." Dan admitted his fantasies about my past lovers, his fear that they'd accessed parts of me that remained walled off to him.

After revealing all this in fifty minutes, we stumbled down to Franklin Street. How, ten years into our marriage and nine months into improving it, could our sex life still be under the thumbs of exes we no longer talked to or desired? We both felt wrung out and dazed. But then we went home and solved the problem, at least at first. We had excellent sex—open, daring, tender, confrontational sex. I think we were terrified not to. Yet once we'd proven to ourselves that we weren't fools to be married—that we could have as strong an erotic connection with each other as we'd had with others before—the backslide began. This time, because we'd exposed the rawest parts of ourselves, the retreat was painful and abrupt.

A few days after that first Betsy session Dan found a box of snapshots in the basement and brought it upstairs, after dinner, thinking he'd show his old self to the girls. Hannah and Audrey snuggled in beside him on the living room couch, all of us together under the enormous peace flag Dan had tastefully framed in pale wood after our fights about wall art. The flag really did look great, like something by Jasper Johns. It was a relic of Dan's parents' counterculture days, red, white, and blue, with a peace symbol in place of the stars.

Lately, happily, our life had settled. Our house was no longer a toddler death zone. Even Dan's cooking mania, when it ramped back up, veered toward homey deliciousness, like mozzarella-stuffed meatballs and spatchcocked chickens. Dinner remained a joy. I stretched my arm across Audrey and over to Dan, eyeing the gray wall I'd painted behind our white kitchen cabinets. That job was one of my final acts in our remodel, and I'd botched it—too impatient to have insured a perfect line between the gray and the white ceiling by applying painter's tape. I didn't know if Dan had noticed. He'd never commented, a small gift, as neither of us had the energy to tape and repaint the ceiling now. But our sweet family moment soon ended. The old Mac power cord box Dan had retrieved from the basement did not contain his old pictures. It contained mine. Among my childhood snapshots (including me, at age six, with my feet on my bike's handlebars) were a half dozen photos of ex-boyfriends—a few of the cereal-selling swimmer, a few of Shane in his ski cap. None were terribly intimate, yet I had saved them. This lingering connection felt like a betrayal—proof, perhaps, that I was like the women who, in psychologist Rowland Miller's 1997 study of romantic relationships, stared longer than average at images of attractive men. This "attending to romantic alternatives," turned out to be a significant warning that a relationship might fail, a better predictor of romantic demise than a woman admitting relationship problems to a psychologist. Dan was furious that I'd saved the pictures. To the girls' great amusement, he proceeded to fling them, sending the snapshots spiraling like Frisbees across the room.

"Oh, Mom's saving a little something for later," Dan said acidly. One of his old girlfriends called every year on his birthday, and another, now divorced, lived in our neighborhood; she and Dan chatted amicably at the grocery store. But this was not the point. I gathered the photos up off the floor, collecting the evidence "that the wife was not really so devoted," as Mitchell would note. Dan had maintained a fantasy of me as almost virginal, without a history, all part of his "defense against the vulnerability of romantic love." This daydream was as common as it was absurd. Still, Dan did not enjoy the bulwark crumbling. He retreated downstairs at 8:00 p.m. By the time I put the girls to bed, he was asleep.

Then, in the morning, Dan e-mailed me before dawn. Neither of us slept well. We'd arisen to work: "Remind me again why you invited so many ex-lovers to our wedding? . . . Also, at the time, you had told me that you'd never slept with two of them. It only emerged later over time that you had. So what was going on there? Not completely ready to relinquish the past? Immaturity? Self-protection? Are you enjoying having a sexual history, too?"

In his novel *Before She Met Me,* Julian Barnes explores the rabid jealousy we feel for spouses' former lovers, as if we expect our partners to have lived in anticipation of meeting us. This jealousy, Barnes writes, comes "in rushes, in sudden, intimate bursts that winded you." It then lingers on "unwanted, resented." This was our experience. The inquisition continued for days. Why had I not told Dan I'd slept with these men? Why had I introduced him to past lovers? Both valid questions, and ones with no satisfying answers. I'd lied during our courtship for the lamest of reasons: I lacked the maturity and presence of mind to tell Dan the truth, that I did not yet think he had a right to know the details of my sex life before him. Early on I felt he held all the cards. Even when I'd marched over to his house on 20th Street and broken up with him, I'd announced I'd be sitting by the phone. The only means I could imagine to grab some power was to keep private some aspects of myself. For a while this strategy (withholding information) had worked. I'd survived our courtship with my self-respect intact. I had not been subsumed. But now Dan was my husband, my one-man band. He'd allowed this reckless poking into all corners of our marriage. He'd stopped seeing me as predictable and boring. The old lie hurt.

"This is the central trust issue in a marriage," Dan said, still angry the next day, knife in hand, mincing herbs to top my lunch. "Can I trust you when you tell me you haven't slept with somebody else?"

The following weekend: jealousy again—or was it an attempt to fuel our renewed eroticism with the required tension? The girls begged us to take them to a carnivorous plant exhibit at the Conservatory of Flowers in Golden Gate Park. Afterward, we all lounged on the thick soft grass, Hannah and Audrey running obstacle courses around the beds of dahlias, Dan and I timing them for "personal bests." A lovely afternoon, physical and sensual. But it incinerated as we left the lawn and walked past the tennis courts to the car. Dan asked whether I'd noticed a well-muscled young man practicing his handstands nearby us in the grass. I'd said yes a bit too forcefully. In some ways, the query was a gift. Dan was allowing for my sexual free agency, granting me my full humanity, acknowledging my life outside of him. Yet the terrain was charged. Nearing an evening at home, we needed to break out of our cozy togetherness—create a gap to bridge in the bedroom, an erotic synapse to cross. Studies by Nathan DeWall and others find proof for the "forbidden fruit" hypothesis—that forcing one's spouse to pretend he or she notices no potential lovers backfires, in the same way we all perseverate when told to suppress a thought. Still, the sexual drama felt exhausting.

"That guy did the epitome of bad-values hypertrophy training," Dan said, grabbing my wrist later that night, pulling me toward the stairs, eager for me to prove erotic allegiance to him. *Hypertrophy training,* in Dan's estimation, was unmanly and vain, weightlifting just to get buff. "You're like a guy admitting he likes fake boobs," Dan said, his voice softening toward flirtation. "And he had chicken legs. Did you notice *that,* too?"

Back in Betsy's office we described the intervening two weeks: the pictures, Dan's anger, the man in Golden Gate Park, Dan's feeling—right out of Mitchell—that he no longer knew who I was. Betsy's eyes looked bluer, more all-knowing than before. She unnerved me with her insight, still I sat in my chair, trying to remain present, as we talked about "rebalancing" our marriage and repairing the wounds I'd inflicted on Dan by being tardy in telling him the truth. The fact that I'd *lied,* that felt huge. But to be honest, I didn't understand the depth of my crime. I'd whitewashed an affair that I'd started and ended before I met my husband—was this such a major offense? To me, it fell into the category of a stupid childish lapse, and this opinion leached into my apologies. I'd said "I'm sorry" twenty times the past ten days. But in my mea culpas I was lobbying, not empathizing. My apologies beaded up like drops of water on an oily pan and rolled away.

In Betsy's office I tried one more time to express regret. "Sweetie, I am so, so sorry. I should have been more candid, really I should have, and I know it's painful that I've ruptured our trust. . . ."

Elizabeth Weil

Dan shook his head.

"You don't really get this, do you?" Betsy interjected.

I turned toward her, startled. "No. I don't."

"That's what I suspected," she said. "You need to understand what it means to the male ego to feel punked."

Dan set upon explaining this with great enthusiasm. My lie hurt not because I'd misled him, but because I'd made him feel unmanned. He'd shaken G.'s hand. He'd invited G. to our home. He'd cooked G. a steak and poured him wine. He'd complimented G. on his pretty wife, and all this time G. knew something intimate about me—that I'd had sex with him—that Dan did not know himself. "What else don't I know?" Dan insisted in Betsy's office, throwing up his hands. "Who else have you slept with? Are there whole football teams of men who've had you and then sat down in my home, thinking, 'Oh my god, this guy is such a punk. He had no idea.'"

Dan knew this wasn't true, but that wasn't the point. I'd compromised Dan's masculinity. Now I needed to help him mend it, so we could find our way back to that less-defended place from which good sex came. For ten years we'd been too distracted to cultivate much of a sanctuary. We'd been busy tending fragile careers, caring for small children, buying and rebuilding a house. But now those careers, the kids, the house felt stable. We could free up part of our psyches to nurture better sex. But already we'd discovered a disturbing pattern: We'd have a great week or two, then stumble, growing tired and less vigilant. Back into the bowling alley we'd slide.

"How do we stay in that alive erotic place?" I asked Betsy near the end of our fourth session—the one we'd determined, at least for now, would be our last. "We have a great run, then we retreat into our shells."

She did not have a simple or permanent answer. "It's a constant process of repair. And you need to make yourselves vulnerable. You need to try."

162

14
Death

I never feared death until I got married. The women in my family seem to live forever. I always imagined I'd be like my mother's mother, Mimi, trying to find the energy to keep putting on a good face decades after most of my friends and my husband had died, bored to tears with my bridge game, my stationary bike, and Charlie Rose. But then Dan and I married. And I started having nightmares. I'd see myself on my deathbed (cancer), scared to leave *him*. In marriage death became specific. I was terrified to face the void, which I didn't think I believed in, without my one-man band.

Our private vows—no cheating, no dying—were only sort of a joke. Dying was the one act we could not survive. It seemed to impugn the very idea of marriage. Why follow a relationship strategy that was the emotional equivalent of putting all one's eggs in one basket and watching that basket when the basket itself—the spouse—could disintegrate at any time? Was it not wiser to diversify (not commit to one man forever)? Shouldn't we spread the eggs—the love—around?

This morbid fear led to my fascination with marriage and death books. I read and reread my favorites, by Joan Didion and Calvin Tril-lin, as well as more obscure titles, like Molly Haskell's *Love and Other Infectious Diseases*. At the beginning of Haskell's book, the author's husband, Andrew, falls unaccountably and suddenly sick, the kind of sick everybody worries about most, the kind in which everything changes instantly, life is upended, and you have no time to adapt or prepare. This is ghastly—that goes without saying. But while Andrew lies swollen beyond recognition in the ICU, Haskell writes of thinking all the chari-table thoughts we all wish we had all the time. "I made deals. I would take Andrew back on any terms," she writes. "I would no longer nag him about reading newspapers all day, or shush him when his voice rose in restaurants. I would cherish his oft-told tales, his doomsday economic theories, the fingerprints he left on the walls and surfaces, the burned teakettles, his absentminded professorisms, his driving."

In this context—fear of imminent loss—her thoughts are expected, even conventional. We will miss everything, or at least we say we will. But it is interesting to consider why. Is there a reason to forgive all, to cherish peccadilloes, when faced with a partner's demise? Is it not just treacly nostalgia? While Andrew is in the hospital, in a state a nurse describes as "as close to death as a person can come without actually dying," Haskell evokes the mess in the closet as "that quintessence of Andrew." She writes that the mess takes on a "holy glow." In "the doz-ens of mismatching tennis shoes, the scuffed loafers, ties fallen from the tie rack, the hangers tumbling out, the socks stuffed in the shoes (one black, one brown)" she sees her husband, his "quintessence," in a way that I was not currently seeing quintessence in Dan's scattered socks, cooking paraphernalia, and weightlifting gear. And in a sense, Haskell's vision is sharper. The mess *does* contain Andrew, his persona—because the mess does not belong to her. It does not belong to their marriage. It is Andrew's and Andrew's alone. The dinners, the movies, the after-noons reading, the pleasant, perhaps even hard-won features of their shared life—these are wonderful memories. These memories might even be called their marriage. But it is the mess, along with the fingerprints and burnt teakettles, that has resisted homogenization, that has resisted *maritization,* if we could make up such a word. Haskell even muses, briefly, about the prospect of remarrying, the idea of finding someone new with whom to go to the movies, pass the sunny afternoons, create a home and share a bed. But she will not find a new partner in messing up the closet. She can't. She's never been a part of that. The closet is Andrew, and as he appears to be dying, it is "the still-warm relic of a saint."

This is beautiful—and confusing. "Holy glow" were not the first words that came to Haskell's mind when Andrew was healthy and energetically maintaining his sloth. She tried to get him to stop. She says as much, explaining, "Andrew's mess had driven me crazy." Trillin, too, writes especially lovingly about his deceased wife's foibles. In *About Alice,* his elegy to her, he constructs her whole character in opposition to himself. He's the goofball; she's the straight man. He wants to spend weeks tracking down "the perfect roast polecat haunch"; she insists on limiting the family to three square meals a day. Trillin admits he's always done this, written a "sitcom" version of his family life, casting Alice as his foil, the slightly buzz-kill mom. But now, in her death, he hits her from the other side, too, giving her a second, teasingly negative and contradictory role: that of the profligate wife. This works because we ally with Trillin. We're swept up in his love for Alice, and in his mind, now that Alice is gone, all her peccadilloes are fantastic peccadilloes. They are her quintessence, her "still-warm relics."

For instance, Trillin describes a night that he spoke at the Herbst Theatre, in San Francisco, before Alice died. During a Q&A an audience member asks Trillin how Alice feels about his depictions of her. And Trillin is honest. He says Alice thinks that they're ridiculous, that they make her sound "like a dietician in sensible shoes." Then this listener asks if Alice is present. She is, and she stands up. "As usual," Trillin writes, "she looked smashing." (Trillin is constantly praising his wife's looks while denigrating his own.) "She didn't say anything," he continues. "She just leaned over and took off one of her shoes—shoes that looked like they cost about the amount of money required in some places to tide a family of four over for a year or two—and smilingly waved it in the air." The shoes, the predilection to keep the family on an even keel—these are the parts of Alice that have resisted Trillin, resisted marriage. They are the parts that have remained separate. They may have been the stuff of arguments, the "small disagreements," to use a term from marriage class, that derailed a Friday night. But now they have a holy glow. They are Alice as fully herself.

So what about me and my marriage to the very much alive and (occasionally) exasperating Dan? I was constantly, if subtly, trying to get him to stop doing things that bothered me, too, to submit more of his outsized personality to our marriage, to me. I let it be known by passive and aggressive means, and a combination of the two, that I'd prefer he talk less about weightlifting, stop treating our family finances as toxic, quit leaving brown socks around the house. But I also knew Haskell and Trillin were right: that I would miss these things most intensely if, god forbid, he were gone.

That joke that we had made early in our relationship, about needing to take more advantage of being two people? That concept had faded into the background, replaced by cracks about "recreational togetherness"— doing activities together for no logical reason. This was the natural ebb and flow of a marriage. Initially, all energy moves toward each other. One has a hard time imagining a friend who is not a shared friend, or conceiving an errand that's not more fun to do together. But then after five, or ten, or fifteen years, the marriage topology, the gravity, shifts. Now every joule of energy goes to protecting that which is separate, in both oneself and one's spouse.

Recently, I, more often than Dan, was the one lobbying for "recreational togetherness," for us to chaperone the girls together to swim class or both pick them up at school. But I also knew I could go the other way: I could singly perform many of our joint functions. A fair number would even run more smoothly. The house would stay cleaner, the kids would get to bed on time; this happened when Dan traveled for work. I even knew, if I ever lost Dan, that I might find someone to take over the tasks that seemed most specific to him: to read my drafts, to protect me from the loneliness of the writing life. Maybe, if I was lucky, I might even find someone to believe in me or to help me believe in myself. But when I imagined this multitalented husband stand-in, I didn't feel relieved. I felt depressed. I didn't want a made-to-order spousal replacement, not even the model with the empathy package custom-designed for the writer with two young kids. I wanted Dan—Dan specifically, a man defined by his prodigious messes, his manic cooking, his unbounded enthusiasm for a barbell coach named Mark Rippetoe, his brown socks.

At some level we already knew this, that feeling captured by Haskell and Trillin, the broad love of the widowed. When Dan was away he'd call and ask, "Do you miss me?"

"Of course I miss you," I'd say.

"But do you miss *me*?" he'd press. "Is it personal?"

15

How Good Is Good Enough?

How good a marriage is good enough? For a long time, I didn't know how to answer that question, when or even if the project should end.

The following spring, after coasting for a while, we drove to the offices of the San Francisco Group for Evidence-Based Psychotherapy. I thought we should at least try cognitive behavioral therapy, as studies show CBT helps married couples more than any other approach. The method is practical and workmanlike. You pinpoint a particular problem. Then you map out new behaviors and thinking processes to break down bad habits. CBT is not focused on mothers and childhoods, the morasses of our personal histories. It's focused on specific actions and patterns, ones you can identify and change.

Both Dan and I liked the sound of this, especially given how our therapy with Holly had concluded. Behind her double set of sound-proofed doors we'd veered into collectively analyzing our individual psychologies. This seemed smart and reasonable: to be a better wife, I needed a deeper understanding of my relationship with my parents;

to be a better husband, Dan needed to grasp the emotional underpinnings of his monomanias. But each becoming less neurotic individually seemed overwhelming—a many-years long, expensive job. Plus lately Dan and I had hit an impasse on a specific issue, one that seemed worth tackling with CBT. As Dan's cooking frenzy had settled, his strength-training obsession ramped up. Most evenings now he returned from his gym exhausted and bad-tempered, strung out on the ambient testosterone and angry rap.

Over the winter we'd made real progress. Relative to Napa, I'd managed to see my own complicity—my tendency to ram through decisions I didn't want to discuss—and this defused Dan's rage. We didn't have skilled conversations, exactly. But ten minutes or an hour or a day after we'd start fighting one of us would say something like "C'mon, we need to do better than this" and we'd work harder to abandon our entrenched posts and inhabit each other's views. I began asking the girls to please wait their turns so their father could finish his sentences. We resisted the slide toward expected sex. We did not always succeed. (It still felt dangerous to be vulnerable with a deadline looming and three baskets of unfolded laundry next to the bed.) Yet sometimes we managed to access erotic intensity without picking fights.

Still now here we were again—another season of delicate poppies in bloom, another therapy office, this one exceedingly tasteful. Our CBT therapist, Cannon Thomas, greeted us looking like a Hollywood agent, in a skinny suit and striped shirt with no tie. Dan and I sat down together in the center of his elegant sofa and explained why we'd come, a well-rehearsed two-step by that point: We wanted to improve our marriage proactively. We wanted to strengthen its weakest links while the whole felt strong. In particular, we told Cannon, we wanted to work on Dan's obsessions and the emotional crashes they precipitated. "I can see a week or two ahead of time that I'm going to crater, and Liz can see I'm going to crater, too," Dan explained. Neither of us knew how to make the crashes stop.

Cannon crossed his legs and propped his yellow legal pad on his knee. "All right, then," he said, light off the Bay streaming in the window behind him. "That sounds reasonable. Tell me more."

So Dan explained how he'd recently cracked again, a hairline fracture along the mental break he'd suffered after we'd lost the baby. This followed a period in which he'd been so absorbed with strength-training that we'd been discussing dead-lifting technique each night at dinner, then watching Mark Rippetoe's barbell training videos on the laptop before bed. Dan had also stopped surfing and running, activities that kept his moods even and calm. We both knew he was augering in—overreacting to insults, sleeping poorly, careening toward the afternoon that, triggered by a call from a disappointed editor, he parked his truck in front of his gym and texted to me "I'm scaring myself."

Wouldn't a good marriage—an optimal marriage—have seen Dan's plunge and pulled him up out of it before this point?

Cannon set down his pen and allowed himself a wry smile. "You're watching dead-lifting videos together?" he asked.

Dan and I both shrugged and nodded.

"Hmmmm, I see," Cannon said, still grinning. Clearly he felt our marriage was not so bad.

And of course it wasn't. I felt deeply connected to Dan there on Cannon's sofa. On our way over we'd even had an endearing near-fight. I'd driven (unusual for us) because as we left our house Dan felt an over-whelming need to assert his autonomy by talking on his cell. Twenty minutes later, as I was circling the Marina district looking for parking, Dan finished his call and set to lecturing me about the legislative riders on the Obama health care bill. I didn't care. I couldn't listen. I hated being late for appointments, and every spot on Union and Greenwich Streets was filled with some gleaming SUV or high-end convertible worth ten times as much as our car. Finally, as I turned down a side street, Dan paused then asked, "Do you want me to quit talking about this for a minute so that you can focus on being anxious about finding a parking place?"

I liked that.

Now, for Cannon's benefit, Dan threw out another problem, hoping to find a trouble of ours that would work for him. "Well, we have this recurring issue that when Liz is really tired she gets really negative and if I'm stressed, too, we get in fights."

Cannon uncrossed and recrossed his legs, not impressed by this, either.

So, after fifty minutes we left, fired as therapy patients, declared too stable to fix for the first time since our project began.

Nothing had changed, really. Our house was still a mess. We hadn't straightened out our finances or fixed our perhaps-goofy stance toward religion. The light fixture above our dining room table still dangled by a knotted cord.

Still, night after night, I slid into bed next to Dan. He often slept in a white T-shirt and white boxer briefs, a white-cased pillow wrapped over his head to block out my reading light, his toppled stacks of cookbooks and workout manuals strewn across the floor. He looked like a baby, fresh and full of promise. In psychiatry, the term "good enough" mother describes the parent who loves her child well enough for him to grow into an emotionally healthy adult. The goal is mental health, defined as the fortitude and flexibility to live one's own life, not as glitch-free happiness. This is a crucial distinction. Similarly, the "good enough" marriage, in psychiatry at least, is characterized by its capacity to allow spouses to keep growing, its ability to give the partners involved the strength and bravery required to face the world.

In the end that's the vision of the good marriage that felt right to me. I didn't want the conventionally perfect-looking marriage, as appealing as that seemed at the start. I wanted our marriage—our exasperating, sometimes-preposterous, idiosyncratic marriage—and the comedown, the humility required to accept this, struck me as the reason the whole project initially had seemed so perverse. It's so easy to misdefine the goals. In the early years we take our marriages to be vehicles for wish fulfillment: We get the mate, maybe even a house, an end to loneliness, some kids. But to keep expecting our marriages to deliver on all of our desires—to bring us the unending passion, or seamless intimacy, or flawless stability we crave—is naive, even a little demeaning. Of course we strain against marriage. It's a bound canvas, a yoke. During the year Dan and I applied ourselves to our marriage, we struggled, we bridled, we jockeyed for position. Dan grew enraged at me; I pulled away from him. I learned things about myself and about my relationship with him I'd worked hard not to know. But, now, as I watched Dan sleep—his beef-heart recipe earmarked, his power lift planned—I felt a wider love than ever.

Of course a month or two later, Dan walked through our front door with a headless, skinless lamb slung over his shoulder. He butchered it with a hacksaw on our kitchen island, and when he finished I sat on a stool, chatting with my husband in his bloody apron, as he vacuum-sealed the parts.

"You know, baby," Dan said, washing his hands, "you've been a great wife to me."

He placed the fourth plastic-wrapped lamb leg in a crate to carry to our basement freezer.

I thought but did not say aloud that Dan had been a great husband, too. I brought the meat down to our cellar. Then, for better or worse—at least for a while—we declared our project done.

Acknowledgments

Many heartfelt thanks to everybody who offered support, wisdom, love, and good humor along the way: Chris Baum, Shoshana Berger, Bonni Cohen, Sara Corbett, Mary Holt-Wilson, Clara Jeffery, Maggie Jones, Lauren Ladoceour, Emily Newman, Hanna Rosin, Sam Stoloff, and Kiernan Warble; Keith Bailey, Ralph Butcher, Deborah Coffey, Holly Gordon, Chad Herst, Betsy Kassoff, Larry Kushner, Ron Lieber, Mindy McHugh, Diane Sollee, Dennis Stoica, and Cannon Thomas; Abigail Walch at *Vogue;* Ilena Silverman and Gerry Marzorati at *The New York Times Magazine*; Kris Dahl and Laura Neely at ICM; Alexis Gargagliano, Nan Graham, and Kelsey Smith at Scribner; my parents, Judy and Doug, and my in-laws, Kit and Dick, all of whom have endless patience; and most important, my incredible husband. I love you. It's personal.

Selected Bibliography

About Alice, Calvin Trillin, Random House, 2006

Against Love, Laura Kipnis, Pantheon Books, 2003

Alone Together, Paul Amato, Alan Booth, David R. Johnson, and Stacy J. Rogers, Harvard University Press, 2007

Before She Met Me, Julian Barnes, Vintage, 1982

Can Love Last?, Stephen A. Mitchell, W. W. Norton & Company, 2003

The Case for Marriage, Linda J. Waite and Maggie Gallagher, Doubleday, 2000

Financially Ever After, Jeff D. Opdyke, HarperCollins, 2009

For Better, Tara Parker-Pope, Dutton, 2010

Getting the Love You Want, Harville Hendrix, Henry Holt and Company, 2008

The Good Marriage, Judith S. Wallerstein and Sandra Blakeslee, Houghton Mifflin, 1995

The Happiness Project, Gretchen Rubin, HarperCollins, 2009

Heartburn, Nora Ephron, Alfred A. Knopf, 1983

Selected Bibliography

Here Lies My Heart, Deborah Chasman and Catherine Jhee, editors,
    Beacon Press, 1999
Hold Me Tight, Sue Johnson, Little, Brown and Company, 2008
The Husbands and Wives Club, Laurie Abraham, Touchstone, 2010
I Don't: A Contrarian History of Marriage, Susan Squire, Bloomsbury,
    2008
Intimate Terrorism, Michael Vincent Miller, W. W. Norton & Company,
    1995
"Let's Call the Whole Thing Off," Sandra Tsing Loh, *The Atlantic,* July/
    August 2001
Light Years, James Salter, Random House, 1975
Love & Money, Jeff D. Opdyke, John Wiley & Sons, 2004
Love & Other Infectious Diseases, Molly Haskell, William Morrow and
    Company, 1990
Love in the Western World, Denis de Rougemont, Pantheon Books, 1940
The Maples Stories, John Updike, Alfred A. Knopf, 2009
Marriage: Disillusion and Hope, Christopher Clulow, editor, Karnac
    Books, 1990
Marriage, a History, Stephanie Coontz, Viking Penguin, 2005
The Marriage-Go-Round, Andrew J. Cherlin, Alfred A. Knopf, 2009
The Marriage Sabbatical, Cheryl Jarvis, Perseus Publishing, 2001
Marry Him!, Lori Gottlieb, Dutton, 2010
Mating in Captivity, Esther Perel, HarperCollins, 2006
"The Mid-Wife Crisis," Ellen Tien, *O, The Oprah Magazine,* May 2008
Monogamy, Adam Phillips, Pantheon Books, 1997
More Perfect Unions, Rebecca L. Davis, Harvard University Press, 2010
The Multi-Orgasmic Couple, Mantak Chia, Maneewan Chia, Douglas
    Abrams, and Rachel Carlton Abrams, HarperCollins, 2002
On Kissing, Tickling, and Being Bored, Adam Phillips, Harvard Univer-
    sity Press, 1993
Open Marriage, Nena O'Neill and George O'Neill, Avon Books, 1972
Passionate Marriage, David Schnarch, W. W. Norton & Company, 1997

Relationship Enhancement, Bernard G. Guerney, Jossey-Bass, 1977

Rethinking Marriage, Christopher Clulow, editor, Karnac Books, 1993

The Sabbath World, Judith Shulevitz, Random House, 2010

The Seven Principles for Making Marriage Work, John Gottman and Nan Silver, Crown, 1999

Spousonomics, Paula Szuchman and Jenny Anderson, Random House, 2011

Take Back Your Marriage, William J. Doherty, Guilford Press, 2001

A Vindication of Love, Cristina Nehring, HarperCollins, 2009

What Shamu Taught Me about Life, Love, and Marriage, Amy Sutherland, Random House, 2008

Why We Love, Helen Fisher, Henry Holt and Company, 2004

A Year by the Sea, Joan Anderson, Broadway Books, 1999

The Year of Magical Thinking, Joan Didion, Vintage, 2005

About the Author

Elizabeth Weil is a contributing writer to *The New York Times Magazine*. She lives in San Francisco with her husband, the writer Daniel Duane, and their two daughters.

Printed in the United States
By Bookmasters